THE COMPLETE GUIDE TO POLICE CYCLING

**Authored by the Governing Board of the
The International Police Mountain Bike Association**

Compiled and edited by Joe Martin and Erik Blair

**Distributed by Calibre Press, Inc.
Northbrook, IL 60062-2760**

The International Police Mountain Bike Association (IPMBA) is a professional association of public safety officers committed to safety, education, and training. An individual membership costs $40 per year. Ever-growing benefits include the IPMBA News, discounts to the annual Police on Bikes Conference, and exclusive access to IPMBA's product purchase plan. In January, 1999, IPBMA spun off from its parent organization, the League of American Bicyclists, to become its own 501(e)(3).

For further information:

International Mountain Bike Association
28 E. Ostend Street
Baltimore, MD 21230
(410) 685-2220 • FAX (410) 685-2240
e-mail: ipmba@aol.com • web site: www.ipmba.org

©1996 The International Police Mountain Bike Association

Fourth printing © 2000 by The International Police Mountain Bike Association

Cover and interior design: Jennifer Horan, Donald Tighe
Copy editor: Melodie Jackson. Photo editor: Andrew MacClellan

To purchase additional copies, contact the distributor:

Calibre Press, Inc.
666 Dundee Road, Suite 1607
Northbrook, IL 60062-2760
(800) 323-0037 • (847) 498-5680
FAX (847) 498-6869
e-mail: staff@calibrepress.com
web site: www.calibrepress.com

ISBN 0-9650262-0-5   Manufactured in the United States

CONTENTS

Chapter Five: Vehicular Cycling

Chapter Six: Technical Cycling

Chapter Seven: Patrol Procedures

Chapter Eight: Bicycle Law Enforcement

ACKNOWLEDGMENTS

Many individuals and organizations have contributed to this work. For their significant contributions, special thanks to Jennifer Horan, Director, IPMBA; Donald Tighe, Director of Communications, League of American Bicyclists; Al Farrell; David Knoerlein; Melodie Jackson; Art Widler; Dean Pangelinan; Robin Miller, past Director, IPMBA; Lori, Yvette, and Joey Martin; and Kelly Arnold.

We want to thank our friends and colleagues for their help in preparation of this book, among them: the staff at GT Bicycles, the League of American Bicyclists (LAB), and its affiliate, the International Police Mountain Bike Association (IPMBA). Without their help, this book would not have been possible.

Additionally, the following agencies and organizations contributed to this book either directly or indirectly:

Hayward PD, CA
Fremont PD, CA
Santa Monica PD, CA
Deland PD, FL
Boise PD, ID
Coon Rapids PD, MN
Las Vegas PD, NV
Ithica PD, NY
Rochester PD, NY
Troy PD, OH
Dayton PD, OH
Pittsburgh PD, PA
Denton PD, TX
Tacoma PD, WA
Vancouver PD, WA
Lancaster PD, PA

Baltimore County PD, MD
California State Hayward PD, CA
Grand Junction PD, CO
Rochester Housing Authority PD, NY
NY Housing Authority Police, NY
University of Pittsburgh PD, PA
Pierce County Sheriff's Department, WA
Alitta: Law Enforcement Apparel
Brat Wear: Law Enforcement Apparel
Creative Exposure Photography
Hank & Frank Bicycles, Hayward, CA
J. Marcel: Law Enforcement Apparel
Shaklee US: Sports Nutrition
US Department Of Transportation
Drake and Associates, Scottsdale, AZ
Washington State Police, WA

FOREWORD

Forget the hype. Strip away the "image," the p.r., and the cliches, and you are left with one fact: The police on bikes movement represents the most effective new law enforcement technique in decades. The arrest records show it; the cost savings show it; officer morale shows it; and community support shows it.

But it has taken plenty of blood, sweat, and gears by a committed core of believers to help the movement become so successful and so fully accepted during the 1990s. Those believers helped build the International Police Mountain Bike Association (IPMBA) into an organization that can help train, certify, and support bicycle patrol officers the world over. The book you have in your hands represents the best of that support.

This book represents the dream of the IPMBA Board: to bring important information to as many people as possible, especially those who couldn't obtain formal training at home or abroad. The dream started in March of 1992, in Las Vegas, Nevada at the first IPMBA Board of Directors meeting, in the restaurant of the Sands Hotel.

At that time, we had sixty members; now we have nearly two thousand members world wide (in countries like Russia, Australia, Iceland, Mexico, Canada, and the United States, just to name a few). I'm proud to say that plenty of other things have improved since then as well.

Then, administrators couldn't and wouldn't believe that bike patrol was an effective policing tool, and in many cases they proved to be the biggest obstacle to getting a patrol on the road. Now, they know what we knew all along: bike patrol bridges an important gap that motor patrol cannot. Department administrators now understand that the void bike patrol fills is as serious as the void between verbal skills and the finality of deadly force.

Today, there is widespread acceptance that bicycles and related clothing and equipment for bike patrol have to be top quality. Many departments learned this quality lesson the hard way, either by buying cheap items over and over or by injury to personnel. As IPMBA grew, manufacturers came to know that we are an important market. Because manufacturers know the value of the visibility and validation we give their products every time we ride out of the stationhouse, our movement has helped make the bikes, clothing, and accessories bicycle-mounted officers use better and safer.

Our training program, the "Police Cyclist Course" has helped officers do their job better and safer all over the world, and much of that course forms the foundation of this book. IPMBA members have personally protected every-one from the President of the United States to the Pope, and the knowledge contained in this book comes from the sweat, blood, and sometimes the lives of people who work as bike cops. The result is the most definitive text written on the subject to date. Although we are now accepted by the mainstream of policing, we must maintain our unity through the organization born out of that hotel in Las Vegas. With a committed organization and a means of communi-cation, we cannot, and will not, ever again be isolated in ignorance. Officers on other beats cannot teach you how to stay alive on the job we do, but other bike cops can and do.

IPMBA has more than a few people to thank for the publication of this text and I apologize for not mentioning them all. If it were not for the support of Al Farrell, Richard Long, and GT Bicycles, this book would still be a dream and not a reality. Thank you, gentlemen; your kindness will not be forgotten. Equally important is the IPMBA Board and others who wrote and edited the material so it would make sense. Thanks also to League of American Bicy-clists staff, past and present (especially Jennifer Horan and Robin Miller), and to past and present IPMBA Directors. But most of all, I must thank the mem-bership. I thank you for having the faith that we could and would achieve our goals, and for supporting our organization with your dues and time. I also thank you for your confidence in me, and the other IPMBA Board Members, to lead your organization in the direction and fashion you choose.

In the spring of 1997, I will retire from the IPMBA Board and will be very satisfied with what we've accomplished since the first meeting. To my broth-ers and sisters who have yet to step forward and make a difference, take this thing farther than any one of us ever dreamed it would go. Work hard so we can say we were a part of something significant in a line of work where it's usually hard to see progress. And finally, thanks to my fellow board members, both past and present, for your guidance, your confidence, and most impor-tantly, your friendship. We did it!

Allan Howard
IPMBA Chairman, 1992 - Present

FOREWORD

B icycles have been around the better part of the last 125 years, but only since the invention of the mountain bike 20 years ago has it become practical for police to consider the bicycle as a serious tool for patrolling (although then, New York Police Chief Theodore Roosevelt put his officers on bikes in the early 1900s, it was a different world then). It's ironic that mountain bikes, which were originally designed to help people "get away from it all," have turned out to be key in the effort to make city streets safer and more enjoyable for law-abiding citizens.

When Israel Garcia (training section coordinator) and Lt. Collie Provence of the Santa Ana Police Department asked me to come down and meet with a group of bike patrol officers and answer some questions about their new mountain bikes, I half expected to be addressing a bunch of guys who probably wondered what they did to deserve this assignment. Let's face it, Santa Ana in the summer-time is sweltering hot! Who in their right mind would trade an air-conditioned patrol car (not to mention the extra protection of bullet-proof glass) for a bicycle?

Was I ever wrong! Not only were these guys super-enthusiastic about getting out of their cars and onto the bikes, they reveled in story after story of successful bike cop drug busts, robbery chases and, of course, the startlingly stealthy approaches on vice activity in progress. One particular set of partners recounted the time they snuck up on a drug deal and busted so many bad guys that they ran out of room in the squad cars to haul them all away. As the bike-mounted officers marched the rest of the zip-tied gang down the block to await transportation, merchants and residents emerged from their shops, homes and apartments to give the officers a standing ovation. Yes!

Of course, bike patrols won't spell the end of crime, but they are and will continue to be an important part of the effort to reduce criminal activity and, perhaps even more importantly, help street officers cover more ground, while being readily accessible to the people and the communities they serve.

All the best...

Bob Hadley
GT Bicycles, Inc.
Santa Ana, California

INTRODUCTION

Until now, those seeking to get a public safety bike unit rolling had to look far and wide to assemble the necessary information. A typical project required hours of phone calls and letters to agencies across the country to ferret out equipment, uniform, policy and training information. You have in your hands a guide that will provide the necessary information to start a bike unit, or help an established bike unit find tips on everything from basic equipment needs to detailed information on policy, maintenance, training, legal issues, and much more.

Some information contained in these pages has previously been published in the International Police Mountain Bike Association (IPMBA) newsletter. The book's title, *The Complete Guide To Police Cycling*, reflects its focus; however, professionals in the security industry, fire service, park service and emergency medical service (EMS) will find almost all of the information useful with very little modification.

While legal definitions vary, the term "public safety" will be used throughout this book, and will serve as an inclusive term meaning police, EMS, security, and those bike units with missions supporting police, EMS, or security. Examples of those bike units include neighborhood alert, crime watch or volunteer trail bike patrols.

This book is the cooperative effort of police and public safety officers from agencies large and small. The majority of the authors are board members of IPMBA, who have researched, equipped and trained bike units. One author has even traveled to Russia to train police officers to use bikes. Our goal was to bring about more answers than questions; we realize, however, that the use of mountain bikes as a public safety tool is relatively new, and rapidly changing. We hope this book will guide you towards success given any future public safety needs.

The Complete Guide to Police Cycling seeks in part to facilitate the return of an old idea: that public safety organizations are part of, not apart from, the communities they serve. The various styles, strategies and tactics which fit under the umbrella of "community policing," suggest that we are service providers, and as such, we must focus on basic values: problem solving, frequent customer contact and accountability. Ours is a people-oriented business, and our tools are merely tools!

One of the more significant problems facing public safety agencies today is the demand for more accessible officers. Departments are struggling to maintain high quality services with limited fiscal and human resources. Meanwhile, the demand for rapid response to emergencies shows no sign of decreasing. Seeking to bridge the gap between personal service and rapid response is the use of bicycles. Officers with high quality equipment and specially designed uniforms can now comfortably meet the demands of rapid response over a surprisingly wide area, while still offering regular face-to-face interaction with the public. It's a win-win situation, indeed!

Many types of public service agencies are being challenged to provide a wider array of services. Portable advanced life support equipment and rescue gear enable bike mounted EMS providers to service patients in remote areas, allowing them to stabilize patients long before transportation is available. Furthermore, public safety needs don't stop at the city limits. Today, EMS agencies, park rangers and rural public safety departments must provide a myriad of services where the bicycle can become significantly useful in delivering those services.

Although we haven't specifically mentioned every mountain bike application possible in society, the concepts, skills and information provided throughout this book should greatly increase the success of any professional organization or individual who decides to use a bicycle in performing services to the public.

HOW TO USE THIS BOOK

The format of this book is somewhat ergonomic. We encourage you to write notes on the pages and highlight as needed. This book has been designed with the cyclist in mind. Its compact size and soft cover fit conveniently into bicycle saddlebags, so it can be readily available when needed. We hope it will serve as a reference, study guide and form of light entertainment.

No part of this book may be reproduced or transmitted in any form or by any means, electronic or mechanical, including photocopying, recording, or by any information storage and retrieval system, without permission in writing from the Publisher. However, using terms and phrases contained in this book to develop or create proposals or department policies is permitted.

In the spirit of professional association and cooperation, the authors have agreed that the proceeds from this book will benefit the goals and objectives of IPMBA and its parent organization, the League of American Bicyclists.

Perhaps the real question isn't,

"Why should we have bike patrols?"

but rather,

"Why has it taken so long for us to start one?"

CHAPTER ONE:
EVOLUTION

1.1 THE WHEEL STORY: A BRIEF HISTORY

The heyday of cycling in the United States occurred during the late 19th century. Bicycles built for two, the "safety bicycle" and women's bloomers were just a few advances to come about because of cycling's popularity. Most people in the late 1800s saw bicycles as a form of recreation. Yet, photographs and historical records tell us that turn-of-the-century police officers used bicycles for quick, practical transportation. So what happened to the bicycle's place in the precinct?

During the 1930s, such police tools as the automobile, two-way radio, fingerprinting, forensics, and ballistics stole the show. A philosophy emphasizing rapid response to crimes and criminal investigation was also moving to the forefront of police thinking. And, heralded as the answer to the problems associated with an era marked by underpaid, corrupt and politically-controlled police officers, "professional policing" was to be the model for a new generation of police practitioners. The familiar beat cop was decidedly unromantic and low-tech in comparison to radio equipped police cars being glamorized by Hollywood.

Like walking beat officers, bike cops never totally disappeared. Although outside the limelight, bike mounted officers continued to operate in beach communities, parks, and small towns.

During the 1960s and 70s, many urban police and sheriffs' departments found bicycles well suited for un-

Fig. 1.1a. IPMBA Logo, top; LAB Logo, bottom

dercover and surveillance operations. Bike officers, however, had just about vanished from city streets until 1987.

A Seattle cop, frustrated by his attempts to get around in traffic congestion, suggested using mountain bikes for patrol. The response in Seattle, now known as a cycling haven, was overwhelmingly positive. Higher arrest rates, positive public opinion and renewed job satisfaction were among the immediate benefits. While the Seattle Police Department was using bikes to overcome Seattle's gridlock, police across the continent were rediscovering "community oriented policing."

Described by some as a return to the values of the 1930s-style neighborhood patrols, community policing promotes that communities must join in partnerships with the police to ensure safe, secure neighborhoods. Departments are retooling themselves to be "user friendly" rather than the sterile "just the facts" kind of police work demonstrated by Dragnet's Sgt. Friday. Competing with these ideals are burgeoning rates of violent crime, and the demand for quick response to 9-1-1 calls. What better way to balance these competing values than with the use of the bicycle? Unencumbered by 2,000 pounds of steel, officers are able to have considerable personal contact with people, while still maintaining the ability to respond to calls quickly—often before a police car can reach the scene. And the benefits only begin here.

NEW SUPPORT FROM AN OLD ALLY

The League of American Bicyclists (LAB), the bicycle's oldest ally, was founded in 1880 as the League of American Wheelmen. Since then, the League has been a champion of cyclists' rights to use the road. The organization supports cycling through special events, advocacy, associated clubs, a nationally recognized "Effective Cyclist" program, an informative magazine, called *Bicycle USA*, and other member benefits. It holds a unique place in the cycling community as the oldest, and perhaps most respected, of all cycling organizations. (Fig. 1.1a).

In 1991, the League, responding to the growing interest in police cycling, was host to the first Police on Bikes Conference in Tucson, Arizona. An enormous success, it led to a second conference, held in Las Vegas, Nevada. During the 1992 conference, the League formed a new branch, the International Police Mountain Bike Association (IPMBA—pronounced informally as "eye-pim-bah") and elected its first governing board from active police cyclist candidates around the nation.

One of the best-known programs offered by the League is its Effective Cycling (EC) certification. EC instructors across the country provide instruction on how to safely, legally, and effectively use bicycles on the road in traffic. In addition to the skills and knowledge imparted to EC students, the program has proven worthwhile for cyclists who have found themselves in court after being injured in a vehicle accident, or otherwise caught up in a legal system favoring the automobile driver. EC certification is recognized as credible, substantive training in safe, legal riding techniques, and League attorneys make themselves available to defend certified cyclists in court. Two EC instructors and founding members of IPMBA, Officer Allan Howard, of the Dayton, Ohio, Police Department, and Kirby Beck, of the Coon Rapids, Minnesota, Police Department, realized that a program based on EC principles that incorporated police tactics would be one of the most important services IPMBA could offer its membership.

In April 1993, after months of planning, ten Police Cyclist Instructors (and eventual authors of this book) from across the U.S. gathered at the 3rd Annual Police on Bikes Conference in Ft. Lauderdale, Florida. There, the first, four-day Police Cyclist (PC) course was taught to 90 American and Canadian officers and constables. The curriculum, adopted as an international standard, included what any officer who works on a bicycle should know about safe riding, police tactics, maintenance, emergency skills and legal issues. New tactics and information are constantly being added to the curriculum.

cient modes of patrol in the various parks and recreation departments worldwide.

Emergencies and Disaster: Emergency Medical Services (EMS) include many job classifications and responsibilities. The question has always been: "How do we locate and stabilize those remote victims without using expensive helicopters?" Of course there will always be a need for aircraft, but mountain bikes fulfill an enormous amount of public safety needs that simply cannot effectively or satisfactorily be done otherwise.

Some disasters require emergency response teams to respond by helicopter. This is primarily due to limited road access, or to fly injured victims to hospitals. However, after earthquakes, hurricanes, floods, tornadoes, or fires, police or rescue personnel have very limited access into the effected areas depending on the extent of the disaster. Bike mounted paramedics and search and rescue personnel could immediately respond to a disaster affected area without using roads that might be blocked or damaged.

Emergency medical services and firefighters, in some areas, could be cross trained to use mountain bikes. Emergency services could send in a bike unit to evaluate and obtain information that could immediately be used to plan an evacuation and manage resources to contain the fire.

Military and Government Law Enforcement: Military police could benefit from using bike units just as city police departments do. Our national security might also gain an advantage using bike mounted personnel worldwide. The military is tasked with an enormous responsibility to guard huge military installations, airbases, embassies, and weapons storage facilities, as well as a number of high security areas such as U.S. Mints, Fort Knox, and the Pentagon. The Secret Service could benefit greatly with a 24-hour bike unit patrolling the White House, United Nations building and other government buildings and national monuments.

Presidential "joggers" can be better protected by cycle mounted agents.

Additionally, the National Guard might have an advantage in managing civil unrest scenarios and disaster response with the added element of a trained bike unit.

Sheriffs Departments: Sheriffs Departments, in many counties across the country, could use the bike mounted deputy in jails and prison facilities, in unincorporated areas of cities, and in rural areas.

These days many Sheriffs Departments use aircraft to locate marijuana fields and direct officers into the area. And in many cases, by the time officers get to the site, the suspects are gone with the goods. The bike mounted drug enforcement officer can cycle right to the site after locating it, thus catching the suspect with the goods!

Furthermore, Sheriffs Departments often are responsible for riot control and civil unrest. Using mountain bikes, deputies could contain and greatly assist in the control of riots and other unlawful assemblies, perhaps not as well as horse mounted deputies, but certainly with less logistical concerns.

Airport Police & Security: Airport Police can better patrol airline terminals, hangars and parking lots using police cyclists. Airports are well known for traffic congestion and crowded terminals, making them prime candidates for bicycle patrol. Bike officers can quickly respond and identify any unauthorized subjects and swiftly patrol the huge parking lots that surround airports. Police cyclists at airports could patrol inside the terminals, as well as the exterior fences and runways. The bike mounted officer has a better view over the tops of cars than someone in a cruiser, giving the bike officer the advantage over car burglars and thieves.

Transit and Railway Police: As in airports and cities, Transit Police Departments have large areas to cover with limited resources. Trains, trams, subways and railways all have limited vehicular access, making a bike unit an effective means of patrol.

Border Patrol: The U.S. border is constantly barraged with illegal immigrants, and the Border Patrol has a severe lack of personnel to control this problem. Here's where a stealthy, quick, all-terrain, unrestricted mountain bike can be very useful. The bike mounted border patrol officer could cover much more area than the officer on foot, and get into areas not accessible to off-road vehicles. Motorcycles make too much noise and are more restrictive than mountain bikes, though they too have their benefits. A large number of bike mounted border patrol officers could be funded for less than a few off-road vehicles.

Housing Authority Police & Security: Housing Authorities are finding that police cyclists can better meet the needs of the neighborhood community than motorized patrols. Housing communities are just mini-cities, thus, they have the same needs as city police departments (approachability, accessibility and crime prevention).

1.3 COMMUNITY POLICING

Community Policing. Whether you are an advocate or not, once you straddle a bicycle, you have taken Community Policing to a new level. Imagine the biggest skeptic of Community Policing that you know. Whether they're a rookie or a 20-year veteran, chances are they are a traditional, reactive police officer who relies on the police radio to dictate their daily activities. If you could put this officer on a bicycle for one shift, you may not change their approach to law enforcement, but you will certainly change the way they police for those eight hours.

Interest in Community Policing has received a huge boost with the resurgence of the bicycle in policing. The police bicycle offers a proactive law enforcement tool that's perfect for Community Policing duties. Before we can examine the specifics of Community Policing on Bikes, we must first understand the ingredients that make up Community Policing.

COMMUNITY POLICING DEFINED

With the birth of Community Policing came a new era of policing. No longer were police officers simply answering calls, writing reports, and then, until the next call, forgetting the problem. The new class of police officers began to talk to citizens, one-on-one, and attend to their fears and concerns. They began soliciting information from the neighborhood about crime, juvenile problems, traffic complaints, deterioration of neighborhoods, poor lighting conditions and more. The police began to act also as a referral service to help citizens with numerous problems that had never been traditionally viewed as "police matters."

Police Departments from across the country advanced from recording problems to solving them—and more importantly, began listening to the public. As a result, police officers became closer to the community and began taking a personal interest in the community, as if they, too, were residents. The citizens began to have input as to where and when the police would use their resources.

Many agencies initiated Community Policing within specialized units and then expanded department-wide. In order for a community policing effort to succeed, it must be accepted and practiced daily by the entire department. It is not merely an innovative law enforcement tool to be applied only by specialized units. Community Policing is an entire new way of conducting the everyday duties of policing. Community Policing must provide the public with daily, decentralized service.

Community Policing Officer is not a title held only by those who wear a uniform. Community Policing can exist within every division in a department. The methods involved in the Community Policing concept can be applied by everyone from homicide detectives to bike officers, and even by narcotics detectives. Every division within a department must enlist the community in solving neighborhood problems and improving the quality of life.

Many officers confuse Community Policing, Problem Oriented Policing, or problem solving as having parallel definitions. The problem solving process is just one of the many components of Community Policing. Many of the biggest critics of Community Policing are officers who do not fully understand its concept.

Many critics believe that Community Policing is nothing more than working on problem solving projects. For some, the problem solving process is too much work. So many of these skeptics are officers who began their careers as reactive police officers, and are happy to continue that way; driving from call to call, writing reports, making arrests and then repeating the process often defines such an officer's daily activities. This officer has little or no self-initiated contact with the public and relies on the incident driven nature of traditional policing to dictate his daily activities. Some officers will grasp the Community Policing concept and others will simply refuse to see its benefits.

Many officers view the problem solving projects of Community Policing as lengthy assignments that take them off the streets. A bulk of these officers believe that taking on these projects transfers their responsibility of their area to the officer working the post or car beside them. Not so. If these officers accept and practice Community Policing in its purest form, it will work in just the opposite manner. Written problem solving reports should, at the minimum, include the problem, short and long range goals for solving it, resources you plan to use, and the immediate action taken. Solving a neighborhood problem may simply require talking to an apartment complex manager briefly about a particular environmental problem. On the other hand, the problem solving process may entail months and months of research, which may be used to lobby for a new law.

One tool used in the problem solving process is the survey, which can be time consuming. Neighborhood surveys typically attempt to gather a resident's perception of crime and neighborhood decay. A survey involving a third of the target neighborhood will generally give you a good idea of what is going on in the neighborhood as a whole. While conducting door-to-door surveys, the officer will come across residents from all social, religious, ethnic, and cultural backgrounds. Surveys should be formed so they are generic enough to handle most backgrounds. The biggest problem that is likely to arise is obtaining a good representation from the residents who do not speak English. This, of course, is effected by the demographics of the neighborhood being studied, and is not always an issue. You may also experience problems finding willing participants for a survey. Attitudes toward the police vary among cultures and may be defined by the way police treat citizens in their native countries. In order to recognize their needs in the community, translate a survey in the native language of the selected group that may become part of the survey. Utilizing translated surveys will promote police relations with people of different cultural backgrounds, and also help reduce fear or crime among particular groups. Awareness of different cultural backgrounds should not be limited to the survey. Cultural differences must be recognized and treated with sensitivity during everyday contact.

An officer, depending on where he works, is likely to come in contact with many different cultures each day. Each culture has different beliefs, values, and norms, and should be treated accordingly. For example, police officers tend to judge someone who does not look them in the eye as dishonest. But Asian and Latino cultures believe it is disrespectful to look an authority in the eye, and people from Arabic cultures believe doing so gives a sign to fight. The list of such differences goes on and on. People of different cultures may adopt some U.S. beliefs, values, and norms, but police officers must be familiar and sensitive to the many cultures that exist in the U.S.

For Community Policing to work, police officers must start using their ears more and their mouths less, and really listen to the neighborhoods. Community Policing requires working together with the public to create new methods and new ideas for solving community problems. It does not matter how petty some issues may seem on the surface. To neighborhood residents, these issues have changed their quality of life. The sole responsibility does not fall on the police; however, the public must also be willing to pitch in by policing themselves.

When not answering calls, or working on an arrest, police officers patrol, patrol, patrol. But studies like the one conducted by the Kansas City Preventive Patrol Study have shown that excessive patrol has little or no effect at all on the crime rate and does little to improve public satisfaction with the police. Community Policing takes that down time to the next level. When not engaged in calls for service, the Community Policing Officer is out in his or her community, talking, gathering information, and discovering the public's ideas and solutions. It is no longer a one-sided effort.

The Community Policing Officer then uses this information to identify outsiders, arrest violators, and remedy the conditions that are causing the problems. It is important to remember that the best problem solving efforts are initiated by the rank and file officers. While the Community Policing concept was initiated from the top, it is put into action and perfected by the cop on the street.

The Community Policing Officer is not just someone who attends community meetings and kisses babies. As Community Policing Officers, we must first be concerned with the problems at hand. Though the public relations aspect is very important to Community Policing efforts, it is but another ingredient in the entire equation. The Community Policing Officer serves as the department's direct link to a neighborhood, and therefore must utilize every law enforcement tactic.

Community Policing has pulled police departments away from the technological advances that have made them incident-driven and reactive. It is no longer desirable to measure policing in terms of quantity; with Community Policing, the emphasis is on quality, personal, proactive service.

The First Ride into the Neighborhoods

The bike has made its way back into law enforcement, not only as an excellent proactive enforcement tool, but as a beneficial means of Community Policing. Bikes have some obvious advantages over their motorized counterparts. The most noteworthy of these advantages is the amount of citizens they enable an officer to come in contact with on a daily basis. It is not unusual for a bike patrol officer to speak with 50 to 100 citizens on a given shift. The majority of these conversations go well beyond a friendly "Hello." Citizens can provide a wealth of information about their neighborhoods and their businesses.

When the Community Policing concept first originated, it was the officers who were initiating the conversations at the businesses, on the street, and at homes. As bike cops began patrolling the neighborhoods, they began being approached in alarming numbers. Citizens started coming off their porches, stopping their cars and walking down the street to talk to bike officers. The police began receiving information regarding crime, fear of crime, juvenile problems and so on, without having to solicit such input. Most importantly, as the bike officer became a regular part of the community, the public's enthusiasm seemed to grow. So what makes a citizen approach a bike officer so freely?

**BALTIMORE COUNTY POLICE DEPARTMENT
TROUBLESHOOTER CARD**

The Baltimore County Police Department wants to hear from you! Help your Police Department tackle crime problems. Let us know about your concerns. Please fill out this card and drop it in the mail.

Problem	Location
☐Drug Traffic	of Problem: _____
☐Graffiti	Times: _____
☐Burglary	Days/Dates: _____
☐Juveniles/Drinking	Comments: _____
☐Robbery/Purse Snatch	_____
☐Vandalism	
☐Traffic Complaints	We would like to get back to
☐Street Lights	you, but you may remain
☐Loitering/Transients	anonymous.
☐Shoplifting	Name: _____
☐Animal Control	_____
☐Vacant Houses	Business: _____
☐Overgrown Lots	Address: _____
☐Gang Activity	Home Phone: _____
☐Other/Specify	Work Phone: _____
_____	(For more information, call your local precinct)

Fig. 1.3a. The problem referral card

No longer does he have to jump in front of a police car, penetrate a steel door, air conditioning and an AM/FM radio to talk to an officer. The bike officer is riding through neighborhoods at approximately ten miles an hour, instead of buzzing through at thirty. The majority of contacts with all citizens have consequently become less confrontational, less authoritarian and less threatening.

The bicycle has also proven to be a tremendously beneficial communication tool. Not only does it benefit the bashful officer who may be timid about approaching the public without receiving a call, but it also encourages the timid citizen. Many residents are reluctant to call or approach officers for minor problems or advice. The bike officer pedaling through town makes himself more available to these types of contacts than officers have traditionally been. This type of spontaneous, face-to-face contact may solve or prevent a multitude of problems. Many officers, after their first shift on a bike, have remarked that they carried on more conversations on that tour than they had in any given day during their entire career.

The bike officer may still encounter residents who are unwilling to pass on information to the police. One way to combat this problem is to make use of a problem referral card. (Fig. 1.3a) The problem referral card is a self-addressed, stamped card that contains a checklist of common community problems, such as graffiti, juvenile loitering, drug dealing, poor lighting and vacant homes. The cards should have a section for the name, address and phone number of the citizen, but leave the option open for an anonymous complaint. Hand the 4" x 6" cards out on the street, or place them on citizen door handles or in mailboxes.

Do not let stereotypes or prejudices get in the way of your contact with a neighborhood. Once you mount that bike, you will be approached by all types of citizens. For Community Policing to thrive, you need the cooperation of this variety of law-abiding citizens of the community. Do not count anyone out, except, of course, the hardened criminal element.

Community Policing and Enforcement Ride Side By Side

The bike is a perfect law enforcement tool when it comes to combining proactive enforcement of the law and Community Policing. In one instance, you may be getting your picture taken with a fascinated child, or talking to a citizen about a juvenile problem. A short while later, you may hide yourself and your bike to conduct surveillance on a possible drug deal. As you round the next corner, you may ride into an armed robbery in progress or another concerned citizen wanting to improve their community. There is no other tool at our disposal that has the stealth-like qualities, speed and maneuverability of a bicycle. The bike allows us the use of all of our senses. As we patrol our neighborhoods, we hear more, see more and sometimes even smell more. The bike is definitely an enforcement tool that does not take us away from the community.

Some bike officers have assigned areas and patrol the same neighborhood every day. Others base their assignments on the current crime trends or crime analysis evaluations. Regardless, bike officers become involved in more informal relationships with the public than anyone else involved in working the streets. It is these informal relationships that allow the bike officer to become an integral part of the neighborhood they serve.

As police officers become more familiar with the neighborhoods they patrol, the bike officer is able to receive a vast amount of information regarding the community and its residents. This information allows the officer to quickly identify outsiders in a neighborhood. Community-based bike officers can learn which family has preschool children and which family is away from home for the entire work day. Information like this, combined with the obvious patrol qualities of the bike, can be invaluable in detecting and preventing crime.

Fig. 1.3b.   Patrolling areas not accessible to patrol cars

A bike officer often patrols in areas that police cars never cover and are sometimes hidden from view. Traditional officers, who may happen to exit their cars, often do so to reach only one location and probably while responding to a call. A bike officer who uses the alleys, back yards and trails that a patrol car cannot reach is much more aware of problem areas affecting the neighborhood. These areas, which often go unnoticed, lend themselves to criminal activity. (Fig. 1.3b). It is important for the bike officer to know where they are at all times. Alleys and walkways in apartment and town-home complexes can make it difficult to know which street or block you are near. To help you serve the community better, ask apartment managers to post addresses and street names to the rear of their buildings. All of those signs we see are posted for a motor vehicle operator to read, and not the bike officer. Having the addresses of private homes, town homes and apartment buildings posted in the rear will also make the bike officer's patrol duties safer.

A poorly lit area, or an area that is in disarray, can be particularly attractive to drug dealers. Conditions like fences that are missing or have holes in them, can contribute to easy escapes from law enforcement. Shrubbery, or even trash, can make it easier for the bad guy to conceal his trade. By detecting and recognizing these areas as potential problem areas for criminal activity, Community Policing Officers can develop long term solutions.

The bike officer has found that it is easier for him to obtain intelligence information from the community than it is for a standard patrol officer. Whether from concerned citizen informants or criminal informants, bike officers have been found to receive a greater quantity and better quality of information. Of course, if a bike officer chooses to ride through a community with deaf ears and blinders on, the information does no good. Bike officers build a definite trust with the community they serve, which leads to citizen contacts from which the entire neighborhood benefits.

Playing Santa

Police departments receive countless numbers of unclaimed bikes each year. Do not let these bikes sit around collecting rust. As Christmas approaches, coordinate with a local bike shop to fix up some old bikes for disadvantaged children in your neighborhood. You can extend this program throughout the year by giving the bikes to kids who have had their bikes stolen or damaged in accidents.

1.4 RESOURCES

Contact IPMBA by calling (410) 685-2220 or checking the Association web site at www.impba.org for more information on resources currently available.

Videos

The IPMBA Firearms Video. Developed by the Tacoma Police Department, this unique policing video demonstrates proven ways to train for situations that require the use of your weapon while on bicycle patrol. $19.95

Effective Cycling. Instruction on how to ride further, faster and safer, confidently, anywhere. Includes bicycle handling and emergencies, vehicle laws and etiquette, roadway positioning, turning, climbing, motorist errors, night riding, and much more. Vital information for all cyclists, novice or experienced. Seidler Productions, Inc., 1992. 41 minutes. $29.95 ($24.95 for League ECIs and IPMBA PCIs)

The Law is for All. Road safety for bicyclists and motorists comes from the four E's: Education, Engineering, Encouragement, and Enforcement. This video is designed to show law enforcement officials and departments the benefits of enforcing traffic laws for all road users equally. Sponsored by the League of Michigan Bicyclists. Blue Sky Productions, 1994. 11.5 min. $14.95.

Videos for Kids

Bicycle Safety First. Geared toward teens and adults. Demonstrates important aspects of bicycle safety, including equipment, clothing, safety checks, traffic signalling, group riding, obstacles, weather conditions, nutrition, and more. Tim Kneelnand & Associates. 13 minutes. $23.95

Bicycle Safety Camp. Geared toward elementary school children, using rap music to stress important safety topics like helmet use, traffic law, position on the road or sidewalk, and being a predictable bicyclist. David Lewine & Associates. 25 minutes. $11.95.

Elephants Never Forget. Animated video targeting children in kindergarten through grade 3. Covers traffic signals, intersections, riding single file, wearing a helmet, passing on the left, and hand signals. Ride Safe, Inc. 7 minutes. $7.95

CONCLUSION

The community oriented bike cop has brought policing back to the basics and the neighborhoods. For those officers who are lucky enough to mount a bicycle every day, morale has never been higher. Everyone knows someone who detests coming to work each day and their performance directly reflects their displeasure. Nowhere in law enforcement is there a tool the public loves, the administration praises, the bike officer is infatuated with, and the criminal despises as much as the bike. The Community Policing philosophy has found a partner with the bike cop, and both are here to stay.

CHAPTER TWO:
STARTING A PUBLIC SAFETY BIKE UNIT

2.1 ORGANIZING AND IMPLEMENTING

A thorough reading of this book should provide you with a good foundation for organizing and implementing a bicycle unit, regardless of the type of application you're planning. The term police cyclist in this section has been used to mean any public safety application. Where specific duties are mentioned that do not pertain to your intended application simply disregard those items. At the very least, consider the following:

1. Do your homework:

    A. Are there any cycling instructors in your area?
    B. Are there any equipment suppliers nearby?
    C. Are there any nearby agencies with bicycle units? (The International Police Mountain Bike Association can put you in touch with bike units and qualified instructors in your area.)

2. Write a plan or proposal that includes, at a minimum:

    A. Financial requirements (see "Alternative Funding," this chapter).
    B. Department policy suggestions (see "Legal Issues," this chapter).
    C. Cyclist selection process.
    D. Equipment needs (see Chapter 3, "Bicycles, Equipment and Uniforms").
    E. Maintenance requirements (see Chapter 4, "Bicycle Maintenance").
    F. Training plan.
    G. Climate and geographical aspects of your area.

     H. Uniform suggestions (see Chapter 3.3, " What to Wear: Uniforms and Equipment").

     I. A mission statement.

3. Once you have the go-ahead, do the following: implement the plan, select officers, write policy, and purchase equipment.

4. Begin formal training of selected officers (cyclists).

5. Continue training and regular maintenance. Consider fine tuning your bike unit by having frequent meetings and training updates and by issuing newsletters. Highlight a section of this book each week, or host an IPMBA Conference to keep your unit's skills and interest peaked.

Hours of Operation

The hours of a bike unit's operation are a much debated issue. It is true that a bike unit should not have the same duty hours as other public safety personnel, but only in the sense that their shifts should overlap other shifts. Then, bike officers will not be used as shift replacements that often, thus increasing the stability of the unit.

By the same token, bike officers shouldn't be treated differently than vehicle patrol officers. Bike officers can do anything vehicle patrol officers can do, with few minor exceptions. Also, it would help to have a specific supervisor for the bike patrol unit.

Here are some additional areas where you can greatly improve your bike unit:

Safety Considerations

Some things warrant repeating. Safety is always important especially during training. If you train safe, then your application in the field will be likewise. Following are some important safety concerns, some of which we've already covered, will cover, or you may already be aware of—but it never hurts to be reminded.

- Always wear a helmet
- Be conscious of motorist blind spots
- Do not ride double, unless on a tandem

- Watch out for opening car doors
- Wear appropriate clothing for the weather
- Use lights and reflectors at night
- Check your equipment before each shift
- Drink lots of water
- Wear eye protection
- Never where headphones
- Use signals: let others know what you're doing
- Crashes happen—even at low speeds on level pavement
- Obey traffic laws unless in pursuit of a violator
- Carry a first aid kit and water

It is very important that you develop a habit of being safe and observant of bicycle laws to provide an excellent example for the community.

The following ten commandments are fitting for any bicycle application:

The Ten Commandments of Police Cycling
1. Know your abilities and limitations
2. Know your bike and equipment
3. Know your community
4. Always be approachable and friendly
5. Always wear a helmet
6. Meet new people everyday
7. Be healthy and fit
8. Be environmentally safe
9. Practice your skills
10. Interact with a positive attitude

Bike Patrol Procedures

Bike officers should concentrate on:

1. The Ten Commandments of the Police Cyclist
2. Community policing
3. Crime prevention activities
4. Patrolling areas not accessible to vehicles
5. Making public contacts in highly populated areas
6. Special operations
7. Parking areas, shopping areas and community events

8. Densely populated neighborhoods
9. High crime areas

2.2 POLICY CONSIDERATIONS

A "policy" provides a framework or guideline for bike units to work within. In established special units, the existence of policy is something the assigned member takes for granted. On the other hand, those selected for bike units sometimes find there is no such policy in place, and no place to look to see if they are "doing things right." People assigned to start a bike unit are sometimes faced with something more fearsome than an armed, drug-crazed perpetrator: the task of writing their bike unit policy.

If your agency does not have a bike unit policy, consider writing one. In a bureaucracy, policies are sometimes written only after a "need" has been identified. And, needs are often identified only after a crisis, like crashing into the mayor on a downtown sidewalk. The result is an "Acute Political Emergency" (APE). The climate during an APE is not conducive to the most intelligent policy making. If for no other reason, authoring your own policy is a good idea because it prevents someone unfamiliar with your unit's operational needs from making up rules he/she thinks you need.

Types of Policy

Variety is the spice of life, and writing policy is no exception. Research your agency's way of doing business when it comes to policy writing. The bigger the agency, the more likely you will have to deal with some kind of committee or administrative unit. When looking into your rules and regulations, consider whether all rules on a given subject are contained in one main "bible" or spread out in several separate documents, with names like:

- Rules and Regulations
- General Orders

- Special Orders
- Policy Manuals
- Standard Operating Procedures (SOP)
- Uniform Regulations
- Standing Orders
- Commander's Instructions

What format and writing style is being used? Consider philosophical, mechanical and style differences.

Look to a unit in your agency of similar size and organizational structure for examples of policies. This could be the fire prevention, motorcycles, K-9, or equestrian units. Read every order, rule, policy, specification, and procedure covering that unit. Ask line personnel and supervisors of the unit for input. What parts of their policies are lacking, or need to be updated?

Overall Mission or Policy Statement

In addition to mechanical and style issues unique to your agency, each bike patrol policy needs to consider:

1. Special or Primary Bike Uses

    A. Narcotics enforcement/buy-busts
    B. Patrol
    C. Investigations
    D. Special events
    E. Community Policing
    F. Replace or augment walking beats

2. Hours of Operation

    A. 24-hour shifts
    B. Special shifts
    C. How your unit's shifts fit with labor agreements, contracts, or precinct MOUs (memorandums of understanding)

3. Weather: Year-round or seasonal?

4. Range Qualification

    A. Shooting with gloves, helmet, and after riding and dismounting.

5. Tactics

   A. Car stops
   B. Vehicle pursuits
   C. Emergency deployment

6. Prisoner Transportation Issues

7. Chain of Command

8. Personnel Selection

9. Uniforms & Equipment. (NOTE: Consider a clause allowing you more leeway in adopting newer, improved equipment when it becomes available, or desirable.)

2.3 LEGAL ISSUES

Prior to 1987, the idea of a police officer resplendent in uniform shorts, patrolling on a bicycle, may have gotten little more than a few laughs in most metropolitan areas. Recent years have seen professional law enforcement journals, general interest print and the electronic media describe the effectiveness of bicycle units in public safety applications. But, as bicycles become more widely used by public safety agencies, the need to address the problem of inadequate and confusing regulations becomes more pressing.

Administrative Actions

Riding a bike is simple right? After all, we rode bikes as kids. However, many adults have a hard time shifting their perspective from that of a child cruising around the neighborhood on their Schwinn Stingray®, to that of an adult riding long hours and thousands of miles as part of an already-demanding job. This may be why some public safety agencies give little or no consideration to policy and the law, and their potential effect on bike unit operations. To operate with little or no consideration of these issues, however, invites administrative or disciplinary actions, criminal fines and civil liability for public safety agencies and individual employees.

Of course, public safety professionals are not going to be careening around collecting moving violations.

Nevertheless there is a saying shared by motorcyclists and bicyclists: "There are two kinds of riders. Those who have gone down, and those who will go down again." Public safety cyclists are professional riders, minus the lycra shorts and big name corporate sponsors. Their venue is riding thousands of miles in areas, and under conditions, most other cyclists choose to avoid. (Fig. 2.3a). Public safety cyclists will eventually crash, but most of these trips to the pavement or dirt will be minor. Training and practice should greatly increase the ability to avoid road hazards and other obstacles. Whenever a civilian's property or vehicle is involved, it almost certainly will involve paperwork. An accident report is often required, where fault or a "primary collision factor" is assigned, thus adding points to a cyclist's DMV driving record. This may cause insurance rates to climb. Find out how cycling accidents effect insurance in your area.

Fig. 2.3a. You wouldn't dare catch a recreational cyclist riding in here

Statewide uniform collision report forms are sometimes used to facilitate the collection of data. The investigating officer of a collision involving on-duty ambulances, police cars, or fire apparatus may have the option of noting, "On Duty Emergency Vehicle." This protects the driver of the emergency vehicle from accumulating points for driving "offenses" that occur out of occupational necessity. Further, it allows the agency managing the reports to capture useful statistics on emergency vehicle accidents. This information may be useful in evaluating training needs and making policy decisions.

Citizen Complaints/Internal Investigations

It is common to see cyclists and motorists interact with each other poorly, or in violation of the other's right-of-way. These chance encounters are often resolved (fortunately) with nothing more than an exchange of unfriendly gestures or horn blasts. These exchanges tend to be fleeting because they are anonymous.

When a uniformed professional is riding a bike, however, the anonymous part of the equation no longer exists. Those making the transition from recreational cyclist to working on a bike as a member of a public safety agency, may be in for a rude awakening. That is, of course, if their off-duty riding habits include cruising through stop signs, weaving mindlessly through traffic, and frightening pedestrians with their seeming lack of caution or courtesy. So, if a uniformed bike cop violates a motorist's right-of-way, not only is the motorist likely to scream obscenities, they may decide to file a complaint with the officer's supervisor. Police officers, even more than the general public, are held accountable for the way they ride. It is, therefore, important that your on-duty riding habits be an example of safety and courtesy. The only exception to this rule should be during the necessary performance of law enforcement duties, and then, only in accordance with established policy and the law. To ride in any other manner invites officer suspension or termination, unnecessary restrictions on a unit—or even its disbanding.

Criminal Liability

The previous section touched on traffic collisions and how causing one could result in administrative action. In accidents involving personal injury or death, officers without adequate legal protection could be criminally charged. The penalties could be as simple as a traffic fine, or as significant as a felony conviction, which for a peace officer is usually accompanied by loss of employment.

2.4 ALTERNATIVE FUNDING

Whether you are establishing your department's first bike unit or retooling an existing one, the availability of funds will be a key element in the equation. Unfortunately, law enforcement agencies don't always have access to unlimited resources. In years when budgets grow lean and departmental divisions must compete even harder for their piece of the pie, funding sources from outside the agency can mean the difference between "do or die."

Sources of extra-budgetary funds are limited only by the imagination and the failure to ask for help. The most productive fundraising effort is one that is well coordinated and organized. Above all, don't be shy. Ask for help, and accept as much as you can get!

The following are some sources and techniques that have proven effective in the quest for extra bucks:

Donations and Grants. Local businesses, merchant associations, and civic groups are traditionally very charitable. When appealing to businesses or chambers of commerce, point out the positive impact of a bike patrol in terms of loss prevention and a safer environment for shoppers. Statistics showing a decrease in retail-related crimes can be extremely persuasive. Homeowner's associations and residential complexes can be compelled to give using the same approach, tailored to their areas.

Businesses and Foundations. Those that benefit from demonstrated crime reduction can also be called upon for donations. Insurance companies, for example, would benefit from a bike patrol that contributes to a reduction in burglaries, auto thefts, and car breaks. The fewer the crimes, the fewer the claims made against the company, and the greater the company's profits.

Colleges and Universities. Institutions can often be tapped for funds. Programs establishing positive links between the institution and the community are usually of interest to college administrators. If the bike unit is being deployed in the area surrounding campus, emphasize the need for improving student safety. Thus, any contributions to your unit will be an investment in campus security.

Federal Grants. Recent passage of the highly-publicized crime bill is evidence of the availability of federal funds for local law enforcement efforts. Federal grants are the most well-known vehicle for receiving funds. However, grants are conditional and require a well-prepared application. Agencies without grant writing experience may want to consult *The Guide to Crimi-*

WHAT CAN BIKE COPS DO TO PROTECT THEMSELVES FROM ADMINISTRATIVE, CRIMINAL AND CIVIL LIABILITY?

• Insist on having adequate initial and in-service training for members of your team.

• Keep records of your training.

• Make certain your agency has a reasonable bike patrol policy.

• Know the law relative to bicycle operation in your jurisdiction. For example:

1. What is the legal status of bicycles in your state?
2. Does the implied consent and driving under the influence statute apply? If so, how do they differ from the motor vehicle statutes?
3. List all the jurisdictions, such as park districts or universities, where you work. Do they have regulations or ordinances restricting use of bicycles? Are there police exemptions? How will this impact your operation?
4. Are there restrictions concerning a cyclists' use of headsets, such as the Sony Walkman®? Do you use radio equipment that may violate any such law?
5. How far to the right do you have to ride? What circumstances allow you to ride otherwise? Can you ride double? When?
6. Does state law or local ordinance require any audible signal device on your bike?
7. What kinds of lights and/or reflectors are required?
8. Are there any mandatory sidepath laws? Do they apply to cops?

9. Is a right turn signal given with the right arm okay?
10. Define the following terms: Highway; Roadway; Street; Road; Sidewalk; Shoulder.
11. What local licensing requirements exist? How do they apply to police bikes?
12. Can bikes be considered, "emergency vehicles?" If yes, are there special equipment requirements?
13. Do you have a policy that addresses the following: when to ride on sidewalks; riding during pursuits; riding in violation of the vehicle code?
14. Are there any training requirements for bike patrol officers?
15. Do your sergeants, lieutenants or administrators understand the legal limitations and liabilities that affect bike patrol operations? Should they? If they do not, who is in the best position to educate them?

- If your jurisdiction does not recognize police/ EMS bikes as emergency vehicles, push for a state law to do so. Minnesota, Tennessee, and California already have laws on the books and can be used as examples.

- Carefully examine the questions asked above and anticipate problems where operational needs may conflict with normal rules of the road.

- Know how bikes are listed in traffic collision reports.

What protections currently exist?

Cops in Tennessee, California, Nevada, Minnesota, and a handful of other states, have taken steps to get laws passed to address the specific needs of bicycle mounted police.

nal Justice Grants by Paul Plaisted (Justice Planning and Management Associates) or *Getting Funded* by Mary Hall (Portland State University).

Bike Clubs. Clubs can also be a source of funds, as well as support. You have a mutual interest, so they are likely to be willing to assist you in a variety of ways.

Traditional Fundraisers. Sales of T-shirts or bumper stickers bearing a "Support Local Bike Patrol" message of some sort can prove lucrative, as well as provide advertising for your fundraising efforts. As with all sales, presentation and marketing are key.

Car wash and bake sale fund-raisers are good ideas, but probably won't generate enough proceeds to be relied upon exclusively. Raffles and auctions of donated items are of some value. Obviously, the more valuable the item, the better the results.

Almost all communities have a fair or festival of some sort. A booth at such an event can bring in substantial donations, as well as introduce the bike patrol to the community. To draw more attention, offer bike inspections and/or bike safety literature at the booth.

Local Newspapers and TV Stations. The Media is a valuable asset when trying to raise funds. Their coverage of your event will undoubtedly increase awareness and response from the community.

Fundraising Rules of Thumb

1. Be sure to clear any fundraisers with your department's "brass."
2. Be certain that donated monies are properly earmarked for the bike patrol.
3. If someone asks you how much you need, tell them— both what you need, plus a small percentage more (just in case). Don't be surprised if they give it to you.
4. When you receive a donation, always write a thank-you note. Also, be prepared to provide a receipt if asked.
5. Develop a "pitch" that is comfortable and effective, but be ready to adapt it according to your experience and to your audience.

6. When writing fundraising letters, avoid generic form letters;personalize each letter to its intended recipient.

7. When applicable, point out that donations can be tax deductible.

8. Tap all resources in your own organization. Officers working in D.A.R.E. and P.A.L. assignments are often experienced at soliciting donations.

9. Try several different types of fundraisers. Don't count on the first effort to produce all the funds you need.

10. Remember, the money is out there. Good luck!

Stretching That Hard-Earned Dollar

Once you have raised the funds necessary for your bike unit, there are a number of ways to make them go as far as possible. Try to find the best deals you can. Assembling and outfitting the bikes yourself will almost certainly cost less than buying a "police package" from a local shop. At the very least, do some research and compare prices. Even if you do decide to do business with only one shop, you'll be able to drive a better bargain.

Learning to do your own maintenance and repairs will also reduce operating expenses. Hourly rates for bike mechanics rival those of auto mechanics. If necessary, find a mechanic course or at least get some experience in a bike shop. For the best response, approach a shop that won't be losing your repair business.

When it comes to fund-raising, be prepared to network, and above all, remember to be innovative, not shy.

2.5 THE IMPORTANCE OF TRAINING

On August 31, 1994, Sergeants Art Hart and Bob Jensen, both certified police cyclists, faced a difficult decision. They were scheduled to work a bicycle beat along Lake Street in Minneapolis' Fifth Precinct where both work as patrol sergeants. Since much of the department's personnel were in St. Paul attending the funeral of an officer killed in the line of duty, they considered trading their bikes in for a car.

But knowing how much they could accomplish on bike, they decided to ride.

Later that afternoon, the officers were on routine patrol through a housing development. They saw two teenage boys sitting on a stoop in an area where officers had received numerous complaints about drug dealing and other criminal activities. Sgt. Hart, who had worked the area for several years, did not recognize the youths as residents, so he decided they should identify the juveniles. As the sergeants rode up, the boys immediately ran in separate directions.

The officers split up, each following one of the kids. Sgt. Hart chased his subject for several blocks. The boy attempted to elude Sgt. Hart by running up and down curbs, through bushes and up and down hills in area yards and businesses. Sgt. Hart, who had just taken the IPMBA Police Cyclist Course, was able to negotiate all of the obstacles and to apprehend the juvenile.

Meanwhile, Sgt. Jensen was doggedly pursuing his suspect, who was also running up and down curbs, through yards, and eventually ran down an alley. As Sgt. Jensen approached his subject, he saw the youth reach into the waistband of his pants. Sgt. Jensen closed on the suspect so quickly that the youth had no time to stop and retrieve the object. Sgt. Jensen simultaneously dismounted his bike and grabbed the suspect as he climbed the fence. The suspect managed to evade Sgt. Jensen's grasp and hopped the fence. Once on the other side he withdrew a gun from his waistband and directed it at the Sergeant. Jensen already had his weapon drawn and quickly fired, hitting the suspect in the arm. With the assistance of a bystander, Sgt. Jensen was able to hold the youth until backup arrived.

"There is no way we could have caught either of those suspects if we had been on foot," explained Sgt. Hart. "In fact, we probably wouldn't have been able to sneak up on them in the first place if we'd been on foot or in a car." Sgt. Jensen agreed, adding, "The fact that

I had been trained as an IPMBA Police Cyclist meant that I could concentrate on my safety and catching the suspect, rather than on trying to ride the bike."

The Case for Training

No other piece of equipment has so obvious a purpose and is so basic in its operation as the baton. Yet, today's police officer is not allowed to carry a baton on duty until he's completed several hours of training in not only baton technique, but appropriate and legal use of force.

Another remarkably simple piece of equipment, and one with an equally obvious purpose, is the bicycle. Amazingly, some people in law enforcement who accept without hesitation the need for several hours of training in the basics of using something as simple as a 26-inch piece of wood, see no need to train bike patrol officers in the use of a machine that has 21 gears and a multitude of moving parts. *(Author's note: there is no recorded case in law enforcement history of either an officer falling off his baton or riding his baton into a parked car.)*

So, if you find yourself fighting your department for adequate training time, here is a list of the top ten reasons police departments should provide both initial and ongoing training for bicycle officers:

10. Officers who work on their bikes wear gloves and helmets that affect the way they handle and shoot their sidearm. Riding gloves are too tight to remove in a shooting situation. Range programs for bike officers need to reflect these differences.

9. The ability to quickly ride through city traffic to reach a crime in progress while listening to a police radio, and then taking a violent criminal into custody without crashing and hurting yourself or others, is quite a feat. It is not a skill developed riding on the bike trail with the kids on a Sunday afternoon.

8. Bicycles, being mechanical, break down. Often this occurs away from bike shops, or during hours that the shops are closed. Knowing how to fix a flat or adjust a derailleur can put you back in service rather than having to wait for a patrol car to give you a ride back to the station.

7. Riding into tactical situations requires that you do something with an additional 30 to 50 pounds of bike accessories that don't fit on your gun belt.

6. Officers exerting themselves all day need to be aware of the demands they are making on their bodies, and how to adjust their intake of food and fluids to remain healthy.

5. Police cyclists must ride down stairs, through traffic, on sidewalks, through parks, on rough terrain, and through neighborhoods that other cyclists avoid, all while paying attention to more than the fact that "it's a nice day for a bike ride."

4. Traffic laws governing the use of bicycles are often misunderstood and wrongly applied by bicycle officers.

3. Lawyers

2. The slow-speed maneuvering required to successfully dodge pedestrians on sidewalks and at special events requires a special set of skills.

   And, the number one reason that police departments should provide training to bicycle patrol officers:

1. It's more exciting than renewing your CPR certification!

Seriously, if your agency deploys bike patrol officers without adequate training, the first time an officer or civilian is hurt, you are likely to become familiar with phrases like, "negligent failure to train," "negligent supervision," and "negligent entrustment." The failure of an agency to provide training for officers who will be using bicycles as a law enforcement tool opens both the agency and its supervisors to tremendous civil liability.

CHAPTER THREE:
BICYCLES, EQUIPMENT AND UNIFORMS

O ne of the most important first steps you must take when developing or perfecting a bike unit is choosing the right equipment. The following tips will help you do so.

3.1 A LOOK AT BICYCLES

T here are many types of bicycles on the market— some of which are not suitable for police work. If you or any of your administrators think you can use a bicycle from a department store for police patrol, pay special attention to this section. The Dayton Police Bicycle Patrol was given several department store bicycles when it first started. Those "gifts" cost more in repairs than would have been spent purchasing several decent bikes. More importantly, they all failed in one way or another, some while being ridden.

Modern gearing gives marginally-fit riders the ability to propel themselves at speeds that, in the event of catastrophic frame or wheel failure, can cause serious injury. This type of failure is more common to the department store bicycle because its materials are generally of lesser quality than appropriate for the demands of police duty. Department store bicycles are toys and nothing more, they're not cost-effective even if they're given to you. These bikes are the Yugos of the cycling world. Similarly, taking a bike out of the property room is the equivalent of using abandoned or towed vehicles to round out the patrol fleet. Bikes used in public safety

Fig. 3.1a. Properly outfitted police mountain bike; also see p. 240

applications are going to be beat up regularly. They will be carrying more and far heavier equipment than that of the average rider. Lives may well depend on the reliability of your transportation, so this is not an area where you can afford to skimp.

There are three basic types of bicycles on the market today: the road bike, the hybrid, and the mountain bike.

The **road bike** is what most people would call a "ten speed." It has turned-down handlebars, thin tires and lightweight rims. Everything about this type of bike is designed to save weight. The racing version of the road bike has a short wheelbase, very high gearing, and is designed to be the very lightest type of multi-speed bicycle. The road bike's frame is too delicate for police work and the turned-down handlebars forces the rider into a position that is less than ideal for patrol work. The gearing on a road bike is usually too high (except on touring models) and the wheels are not nearly durable enough.

The **hybrid bicycle** was born after the mountain bike to cater to the non-cycling adult public. It was designed to be a combination of the road and mountain bike. As with many things in life, anything that attempts to specialize in more than one thing, usually does neither well.

The hybrid looks like a mountain bike, but a close inspection reveals that the tires and rims are thinner than those of a standard mountain bike. The 26-inch diameter wheels used on a mountain bike are stronger than the 700C wheels used on a hybrid. 700C tires are not appropriate for public safety use.

The component quality on a typical hybrid is usually below a police department's required minimum. Hybrids are designed to be sold at a lower price to adults who don't have a lot of cycling experience.

The **mountain bike** is the best type of bike for police patrol. More specifically, a mountain bike in the mid- to high-end of most product lines is best suited for public safety work. (Fig. 3.1a; also see p. 240). The high-quality mountain bike has no rival when it comes to overall strength. Its durability comes from the combination of stronger (yet lighter) materials, closer tolerances in the components, and a frame made of tubing specifically designed to endure the physical stresses put on the bike by hard aggressive off-road riding, while keeping the overall weight lower than a high tensile steel bike.

Since mountain bikes were designed to be used off-road and away from the local grocery or bike shop, provisions had to be made to permit the rider to carry items essential for a trip into the woods. These provisions are in the form of "braze-ons" which are threaded tabs welded to the frame, permitting the attachment of water bottle cages, rear racks, and fenders. This added equipment is definitely essential for public safety uses where considerable amounts of gear and equipment is carried—sometimes in the neighborhood of 10 - 15 extra pounds. Here again is another reason to select the lighter, mid- to high-end mountain bike over the typical department store bike that weighs in at about ten pounds heavier without the added equipment. You'll definitely feel the difference on a long, uphill grade.

The mountain bike's rims, as mentioned earlier, are smaller in diameter than its road and hybrid counterparts, but are also wider, which enables a wider tire to be mounted. The wider tire can be useful in absorbing road shock by adjusting tire pressure according to the rider's liking, as well as offering more traction due to more rubber contact with the pavement. (See section 3.2 on Bike Parts and Accessories for an explanation of frame materials, wheels, components, etc.).

The range of gearing on the modern mountain bike allows most riders to climb the steepest of hills while also providing the gear combinations needed for high-speed call responses or pursuits. The gearing can also be tailored to match the special needs of specific patrol areas. For example, if you patrol a mainly urban jurisdiction with relatively flat landscape, you might want to change the number of teeth on the large chainring to

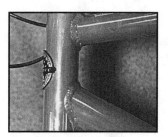

Fig. 3.2a. TIG welded frame

provide a "taller" ratio similar to a road bike for faster pursuit riding. Conversely, you might want to lower the number of teeth on the middle and small chainrings if you work in a hilly locale, to give a lower gear ratio making hill climbs easier and less fatiguing. Check with your dealer to see if the "police special" you order already has some of these gear changes specified (spec'ed) as original equipment for public safety applications.

Finally, the riding position of most mountain bikes is more suited for long hours in the saddle because you sit in a more upright position, putting the bias of your body weight on the saddle and your butt, instead of your arms and hands. Of course, this holds true only if you're riding the correct frame size for your body and have the saddle and stem properly adjusted. Generally, the saddles on mountain bikes are also wider and more absorbent of shock than other models of bicycles, insulating the rider from most jolts and jars from rough terrain.

3.2 BICYCLES—FRAMES AND COMPONENTS

Frames

S tarting at the mid-price range with mountain bikes usually puts you into a high-quality frame. Because the frame is the very heart of a bicycle, concentrate on buying a bike with a high-quality frame. All the high-end parts in the world won't cure an inferior frame. When on a budget, pick a bike that has a good frame and medium-priced components. Common types of frame construction for this range of bikes include:

TIG Welded Cro-moly Steel. This is steel alloy tubing that has been tig welded. TIG stands for Tungsten Inert Gas welding. (Fig. 3.2a). This joining process involves heating the joint with an electric arc. The area becomes so hot, the tubes actually fuse together. A steel filler is added to effectively produce the desired joint size and shape. The actual tube-to-tube bond guarantees integrity in the joint. When the steel is molten, it's prevented from reacting with oxygen by flooding the work area through the torch with an inert gas like argon. TIG welding is normally used on steel, aluminum, or titanium tubes. Steel is a tried and true performer; it rarely fails catastrophically. Cro-moly is a lightweight steel alloy containing chromium and molybdenum that is far superior to the grade of steel used in low-priced bikes.

Fig. 3.2b. Lugged frame

Lugged Cro-moly Steel. Brazing is one of the more traditional ways of joining frame tubes together. Tubes are fit into sleeves called lugs and the entire joint area is heated with a torch. Silver or brass is then added to the joint. This molten material cools, hardens and joins the tubes together. (Fig. 3.2b).

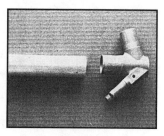

Fig. 3.2c. Aluminum frame before bonding

TIG Welded Aluminum. TIG welded aluminum involves the same process as the TIG welded steel described above. TIG welded aluminum frames usually use oversized tubing. Only certain grades of aluminum can be welded, other grades must be bonded. Aluminum has several advantages over steel. Aluminum won't rust, and it has the ability to absorb some road shock without transmitting it to the rider. Aluminum's down side is that once the frame is crimped or damaged, it cannot be repaired, only replaced. However, most reputable manufacturers will replace a failed frame. Check the warranty before you buy.

Fig. 3.2d. Un-glued bonded frame

Bonded Aluminum. This process uses aluminum tubes that are glued to frame lugs with space-age adhesives. (Fig. 3.2c). The stated advantage of bonding is precise frame alignment. While the glue is cured, the frame remains in a jig that maintains proper alignment. This typically isn't a problem, however, because these frames are re-aligned (coldset) after the joining process.

Some bonded aluminum frames literally can come un-glued, however. (Fig. 3.2d). Bonding ferrous and nonferrous metals together can sometimes lead to joint failure. A manufacturer who uses this process claims their failure rate is minuscule compared to the number of frames they produce. The rider of a bicycle that comes un-glued at the headtube and falls to the ground is likely to be less cavalier about this minuscule failure rate. Nonetheless, failure of a bonded aluminum frame that utilizes aluminum tubes AND lugs is almost unheard of.

There are other frame materials such as carbon fiber and titanium, but these materials are better suited for recreational use and competition where minuscule weight savings are deemed important. These materials have a very high cost compared to the materials previously outlined. And, they are still on the cutting edge of technology—which is another way of saying they have not met the test of time. Bicycles used for patrol are punished worse than some bicycles used by professional racers. While you don't want a Yugo for a patrol car, you don't really need a Rolls Royce either, and that's what these hi-tech materials equate to.

Components

The bicycle components you will most often come across are manufactured by Shimano (which currently maintains more than 90 percent of the market share), Campagnolo (called "Campy" in bike circles and famous for high-quality road bike components), and Sun Tour (which went out of business in 1995). The components of all three manufacturers are viewed as good-quality products; just start in the middle range and look up the product line. Reading bike publications and hanging around bike shops are both great ways to become familiar with the range of quality within each product line. Although Shimano completely dominated the componentry market in mountain biking's first decade, other manufacturers are increasingly carving out a high-end niche in the market.

The "components" of the bicycle are mainly the drive train and braking equipment installed at purchase, whether by your local bike shop or from the factory. Typically these include: the front and rear derailleurs; rear freewheel- or cassette-cogs; shifter devices;

chainrings and crankarms; chain; wheel hubs and rims; brake levers; cantilever brakes and pads; and all cables. For the most part, bicycle manufacturers will install, or "spec" (specify) components as a complete group of parts designed to work compatibly with each other. These groups are tiered in order of quality, precision, and, ultimately, their longevity. Obviously, higher precision parts made of higher quality materials will outlast those at the lower end of the tier.

There are a few manufacturers beginning to mix brands and tiers of components on the same bike to lower the "price point" to boost sales. There is nothing wrong with that approach to marketing, since most manufacturers are tuned in to the tier of componentry needed to endure the perceived level of abuse and riding ability of a target consumer group. However, a word of caution is needed for the buyer of that bike for police patrol purposes.

In spec'ing a combination of lower- and middle-tier components on mid- to lower-priced bikes, the police buyer may "get a good deal" on the unit, but probably will be short-changed as a result by having to replace the lower-tier parts sooner than the manufacturer anticipated for the target consumer of the bike in that price range. Consequently, it is more cost effective to buy a bike in the mid-to upper-price range with a complete group of parts—at least the drivetrain parts—than to buy mixed parts. The exception here would be that the seller understands the purposes for which the bike is being purchased—there are many "higher-end" bikes with mixed componentry designed for the rigors of heavy off-road use and racing. All of these bikes are suitable for police use.

While an individual can afford to be eclectic in mixing and matching parts, if it's a "company-owned" fleet of bikes you are buying, you're better off choosing a "group" (or "groupo" if you're an aficionado) of components. Keep in mind that, often, as you near the top of a component manufacturer's product line, there may be little or no discernible difference in performance between the top two or three derailleurs, or hubs, for instance. The structural difference between like components is usually in the materials some pieces of the components are made of. For example: a manufacturer may substitute a plastic bushing for one made of a higher-grade nylon version, which may have a longer life span; or, the chainrings may be made of steel, rather than the lighter alloy models. The difference between the most expensive part and the next lower—or even next lower to that—may be purely cosmetic, or a difference in weight. The bottom line is: Do some research before you buy!

Shifters

Although you may not have a choice when you decide on a particular model bike for patrol work, there are several options regarding the types of shifter mechanisms on the market for mountain bikes. With all models of shifters, the left shifter controls the front derailleur and the right controls the rear derailleur. With few exceptions, shifters on modern mountain bikes are "indexed," meaning that each time the shift mechanism is moved to change a gear, it clicks into a semi-fixed position that alligns the derailleur and chain precisely in line with the selected freewheel gear/cog. This accurate alignment ensures smooth shifting and prevents premature wear of the chain and gears/chainrings. Not all front shifters are indexed because it is sometimes necessary to "feather" the lever back and forth to keep the front derailleur cage from rubbing against the chain as the angle of the chain changes during rear cog shifts. However, most newer models will down-shift in an indexed mode.

The older—but still preferred by many—model is the "above-the-bar" thumb shifter, which shifts gears by using the thumbs (and first fingers) to move the levers.

Gearing

The typical gearing setup for mountain bikes is a 24-36-46 crankset and a 12-28 seven-speed rear cassette, yielding a 22-inch low gear and a 99.7-inch high gear. Because we use the bikes on the street, we don't need gears quite that low. The optimum setup for police work is a 28-38-48 crankset and a 12-28 cassette. That gives us a 26-inch low gear and a 104-inch high gear. The cranksets that come equipped on the majority of mountain bikes are 175mm long. Consider equipping bikes with 17-inch frames or less with 170mm crankarms. Bikes with 18-inch frames and larger should use 175mm cranks.

Wheels

Wheels should be built for strength because they take a lot of abuse and are the only thing between you and the ground. Try to save some money here, and you will probably pay later. Hubs should have a minimum of 36 holes for spokes because the more spokes you get in the wheel, the less it will need to be "trued" or straightened. Wheels should be laced in a "3 Cross" fashion, meaning each spoke should cross another spoke 3 times between the threaded and hooked ends.

Spokes should be stainless steel, 14g straight gauge. Straight gauge spokes are the same thickness throughout the spoke's entire length. Double-butted spokes are thicker on the ends and thinner diameter in the middle to save weight. Police mountain bike wheels should be designed for strength first, weight savings second.

Rims should have double-wall construction and be at least one-inch wide. Mountain bike tires are generally quite wide. If you use a wide tire with a narrow rim you risk poor tire performance.

Narrow rims may also cause cantilever brake shoes to drag on the sidewall of the bulging tire, which causes tire failures. On the other hand, if you use a wide rim and a narrow tire, you will surely damage the rim because the narrower tire will flatten out trying to span the distance of the rim, offering it little or no protection.

Anodized vs. Non-Anodized Rims

Some manufacturers spec anodized rims on their bicycles, and suggest that added strength is achieved by this surface treatment. In fact, no useful effects other than aesthetic results are achieved. Anodized rims can usually be spotted because they're a different color than aluminum. This may not always be the case though; there are anodized rims that are silver and look just like non-anodized versions. Anodized rims are not any stronger than non-anodized rims when all other things are equal, and they have a diminished braking performance in comparison to non-anodized versions.

Hard anodizing is also a thermal and electrical insulator. Because heat is generated in the brake pads and not the rim, braking energy must cross the interface to be dissipated in the rim. Anodizing, although relatively thin, impedes this heat transfer and reduces braking efficiency by overheating the brake pad surfaces. Fortunately, in wet weather, road grit wears off the sidewall anodizing faster than non-treated rims, leaving a messy looking rim with a better braking surface.

Anodizing has nothing to do with heat treatment, does not strengthen rims, and costs more to boot.

Tires

The knobby tires that come on the mountain bike are not suitable for pavement use. They're noisy and not enough of the tire contacts the ground, especially when it's wet. Riding a stock knobby tire on the street when it's wet is about like riding on ice. If you make no other change to a mountain bike for public safety work, make sure you change the tires. Models of tires that seem to work best for police work are those designed for street use, and that have Kevlar belts built into the tires to minimize flats. These tires usually have a smooth tread surface with "sipes" (thin grooves) running from the center of the tread to the outer edges. These are for channeling water out from under the contact patch to prevent hydro-planing in wet conditions.

However, for riders whose patrol area includes paved and un-paved terrain, or anywhere varying traction requirements are present, multi-purpose tires (combination on- and off-road) are a good choice. These tires generally have a center "rolling ridge" for smooth pavement riding, surrounded by a series of moderate lugs (knobbies) for off-road traction. (Fig. 3.2e). The overall profile of the tire is rounded to eliminate the poor handling characteristics of a full-fledged off-road knobby tire on pavement.

Fig. 3.2e. Many mountain bike tires are available, from traditional "knobbies" to road combination tires

Flat resistance is an important consideration for public safety bicycles and there are several options available. Tires with Kevlar belts built into the tread are an excellent way to cut down on punctures; or "tire liners" made of a nylon or flexible plastic can be inserted between the tube and the tire to accomplish the same thing. In addition, self-sealing liquids can be put in the tubes to fix punctures as they happen, and will usually fill the hole before the tire loses much air. Tubes with self-sealing liquids are also very effective in keeping you on the road and out of the repair shop. The downside of all of these measures is the additional weight they add to the wheels on an already heavy bike. This is a trade-off necessary for reducing the chance that you won't make it to the call in time.

Pedal Retention Systems

Something that attaches your foot to the pedal is a necessity. Not only does it make pedaling more efficient with less effort, but it keeps the foot securely on the pedal to prevent injury. There have been some nasty injuries resulting from a foot that slipped off a pedal. This may be the hardest thing for novice cyclists to adjust to; but if you choose the right pedal retention system you will master it in no time.

Toe clips and straps are the oldest form of pedal retention systems and they still perform fairly well. The big problem with clips and straps in police work is that you can't tighten up the straps and receive the full benefit of pedaling efficiency due to the need to be able to quickly and easily remove your foot from the pedal. This eliminates one of the advantages of a retention system.

Clipless pedal systems have been designed with the mountain biker in mind and for the most part, these are good systems. Systems designed for road riding do not allow you to walk normally and cannot be used for public safety applications. Your foot is attached to the pedal via a plastic or metal cleat inside the sole of the riding shoe. When you want off the bike, all you have to do is rotate your heel outward and the pedal releases your foot. The cleat is positioned inside the sole of the shoe so that it can be used for walking or running. One drawback to this system is that novice riders may have trouble inserting and releasing their feet. This can be overcome with practice. (See Section 3.3 "Footwear" for more on cleated shoes).

Handlebars

Over long periods of time the hands can go numb using standard one position mountain bike handlebars. Constantly changing your hand position will relieve numbness and reduce the chance of permanent injury to the tendons in the wrist. Handlebars that have curved ends extending past the grips, and the clamp on accessory "barends", allow for a number of hand positions are available, and assist immensely in climbing hills. But they can pose a problem in tight maneuvering situations and also give a suspect an opportunity to gain leverage over your bike. The hooks or curved ends of the bars should never be pointing straight up. They should always be at a forward, upward angle away from the rider, to prevent injury during an unexpected trip over the bars.

Racks and Bags

Because police work involves mountains of paperwork a rear rack and bag are mandatory. Consider using a welded aluminum rear rack and a variety of soft-sided rear bags. Many are somewhat water resistant and have expandable sections that become available by opening a zipper. Other features include outside storage pockets and a clip on strap, allowing the bag to be carried in on a call.

"Hard-shell" plastic, rack mounted, trunks have the advantage of being completely waterproof and offer a more secure locking ability than a soft bag. But they may not be as utilitarian because they lack the expansion capability of the soft bag, and if not properly designed—or prepared by the rider—the contents will rattle. In addition, the case itself could eventually fail where it's bolted to the rack, due to the constant vibration unless, of course, precautions are taken when mounting the unit initially (rubber grommets or padded washers will usually alleviate this problem). And finally, the hard case cannot be easily removed from the bike should you need it and its contents to accompany you on a call.

Water Bottles

Two water bottles and cages are optimum, but one will do. Use good quality one-piece aluminum cages. Super lightweight bottle cages made of other materials are a gimmick. Though they are more expensive, they don't hold the bottles as well. Bicycling is a very ad-oriented sport, so be careful not to use water bottles with logos from companies that produce pharmaceutical drugs or alcohol. This is detrimental to other departmental programs like D.A.R.E. A cheap trick that will keep your water cold in hot weather is to keep a wet sweat sock over the outside. The evaporation of the water in the sock refrigerates the water inside the bottle. A dark color is less noticeable and it shows less dirt than a white sweat sock.

Kickstands

A kickstand is a must on a police bicycle. The kickstand is usually mounted on the chainstays behind the bottom bracket. Because a standard kickstand is located near the middle of the bike, the weight of a rear bag may cause the bike to tip over. For this reason use a kickstand that attaches to the cross section of the left rear chainstay and the

WATER: THE CRUCIAL LIQUID

Basic Information About Hot Weather Riding

Some Facts:

- A typical adult loses about one to two liters of fluid per hour working or exercising outdoors in extreme temperatures.

- People have notoriously poor thirst sensation, so by the time you feel thirsty, you have already started to become dehydrated.

- Drinking copious amounts of liquids when the mercury soars, whether or not you feel thirsty, seriously decreases the chances of dehydration.

- Extreme heat affects the brain, impairing judgement and producing confusion that may mask the true nature of the problem. In conditions of extreme heat and high humidity, organ functions are seriously disrupted and crucial cells and proteins in the body break down.

- The brain controls body temperature. The control center is the hypothalamus, which monitors temperature signals from internal organs as well as the skin, limbs and blood. When the external temperature is above the body's normal 98.6 degree temperature, the hypothalamus alerts the body, stimulating sweat glands and dilating blood vessels in the skin. Profuse sweating begins, the first step of overheating. A little sweating is acceptable; however, excessive sweating can lead to lack of fluids, causing blood pressure to drop, and causing the body's finely tuned mechanisms for regulating temperature and cooling to start malfunctioning. This can lead to heat exhaustion or even to heatstroke.

Heat Exhaustion:

- Heat exhaustion occurs when the body runs short of water and salt.

- The initial symptoms are: face is pale; headache; nausea; cool skin, clammy; sweating profusely; disorientation and confusion are common.

- The later symptoms are: collapsing; heatstroke.

- First aid: find cool shade; drink water with two teaspoons of salt per liter.

- Precautions: drink a lot of water; get enough salt; stay in the shade as much as possible.

Heatstroke:

- Heatstroke occurs when the body's sweating mechanism breaks down and the body overheats.

- The initial symptoms are: face is flushed; headache; nausea; skin hot and dry, no sweating; body temperature is 104 or higher.

- The later symptoms are: confusion, shock and coma.

- First aid: cool victim down immediately; place in shade; wrap in cool, wet sheet; call medical assistance. If heatstroke is not treated, damage to organs and cells can occur, resulting in death.

- Precaution: drink a lot of water; get enough salt; stay in the shade as much as possible.

Basic tips for hot weather riding:

- Dramatically increase your intake of water, especially before, but also during, your patrol.

- Have two water bottles on your bike, filled to the brim with icy water. Drink eight ounces every fifteen minutes. The bare minimum is at least one water bottle (32 ounce) Keep in mind your own body needs. Be sure, however, to drink slowly; drinking large amounts of water quickly could cause cramps.

- Avoid sugary and caffeinated beverages.

- If at all possible wear clothing that will whisk sweat away from your body, keeping your body temperature low.

- If riding in extreme heat, you begin to feel nauseated or dizzy, find a cool spot and slowly drink water. Also, if possible, plan stops in cool areas, either in shade or in air conditioning; this will cool your body temperature.

- Eat something light before going on patrol. Salads and fruit help replenish fluids, while meat and other high-protein foods increase the body's metabolic rate. Significant water is required to digest protein, thus eliminating your body's necessary water supply.

- Drinking commercially available electrolyte drinks does help on a long term basis because these fluids are maintained in the body longer than plain water. However, do not use them as a substitute for plain water.

speed measuring devices have made their way into the 20th century with the invention of the cyclometer. The cyclometer is a small computerized speedometer that is attached to the center of a bicycle's handlebars and has either a wired or wireless magnetic sensing unit on the front or rear wheel.

Each time the wheel's magnetic sensor makes one complete revolution past the sensing unit mounted on the bicycle's frame, it is registered on the cyclometer. When the cyclometer is installed it must be calibrated with the proper wheel circumference. A digital display features such measurements as current speed, maximum speed, average speed of the trip, elapsed time, time of day, trip miles and current odometer mileage. Many cyclometers may be toggled to display mph or kph, some even display pedal RPM, which is useful for training.

Some computers are "intelligent" enough to sense when the wheel is not turning and shut down the average speed and elapsed time functions until the bicycle is moving again. Computers can be useful in keeping daily mileage statistics or for scheduled bike maintenance.

3.3 WHAT TO WEAR: UNIFORMS AND EQUIPMENT

The police bicycle has been called the "stealth fighter" of police work. Stories abound of suspects being taken completely by surprise when descended upon by bike cops. This underscores the need for bicycle officers to be quickly and unquestionably identified as law enforcement officers. Traditional uniforms are obviously not well adapted to the physical demands of this mode of transportation. So called "tactical uniforms" also fall short of the bike officer's need for functional clothing. Appropriately balancing safety, comfort and professional appearance is the challenge faced by any agency putting its officers onto bikes. This

THE CYCLOMETER: AN AID IN ACCIDENT RECONSTRUCTION

For the reconstructionist who is trying to determine the speed of a bicyclist, a computer that will record average and maximum speed would appear to be an asset.

Most of the computers, also called cyclometers, will have two buttons. One is to start and stop all functions, the other is used to select the current mode. Sometimes the buttons will actually be labeled "mode" and "start/stop." The start/ stop button is used much like a trip meter on a car: when the trip begins you hit start and when the trip ends you hit stop. If the computer remains running after the trip is over it will eventually bring the average speed reading down to "0" mph if the wheel is not turning.

The "mode" button toggles the computer's screen between the various functions. Usually you can push the "mode" button one click for each mode until it's been toggled into the maximum or average speed position, whichever is preferred. Never push both the "start/stop" and the "mode" buttons at the same time. This will almost always clear the computer's current readings. Almost every cyclometer is removable from its handlebar mount so there is no reason to continually push buttons on a cyclometer that you are not at least a little familiar with. Take the cyclometer off its mount, go to a bicycle shop, and let them show you how to display the readings without destroying the data.

A file of user manuals for the wide variety of computers that have the functions that would assist you as a reconstructionist in determining speed would put you one step ahead of the game in this high-tech world.

Average speed, whether reflected in mph or kph, is the distance a rider would travel in one hour at their current pace. Maximum speed is the fastest speed that a rider has traveled for a particular ride, which is also expressed in either mph or kph. Both of these functions reset to "0" when the cyclometer is reset.

Cyclometer manufacturers boast of 99.9 percent accuracy, which is more accurate than some car speedometers. There are several circumference settings in a cyclometer owner's manual for each wheel and tire size. But if the manufacturers' claimed 99.9 percent accuracy rating is to be obtained, the bicycle must be rolled over a prescribed distance while supporting the weight of the rider. If a rider does not wish to do this, they can use one of the existing wheel/tire combination formulas in the owner's manual and still obtain a fairly accurate reading.

section attempts to address most of the uniform questions faced by new bike units and present some things to consider for units already in operation.

As bike patrols have grown in number, becoming a large, specialized segment of public safety, so have manufacturers of bike specific uniforms and equipment. Bike patrol units under fiscal constraints obviously must make due with what is cost effective for their program, which may mean a modification of standard uniforms, such as cut-off pants or shorts. However, the difference in quality between modified, standard uniforms and bike specific uniforms is worth budgeting for as soon as is practical.

The guiding philosophy of designing bike cop uniforms should be "operational necessity." The world is a diverse place. What works well in Maine may not work in Las Vegas. And, a great idea in one place may even be illegal in another. Uniforms are no different.

A pitfall some agencies experience when designing bike uniforms is the temptation to change the uniform drastically from their regular look, for no other reason than because somebody thinks it looks "cool." Non-riding officers may well resent any "special" exemptions bike officers get unless there is an articulated reason for the change. Officers who work on motorcycles, horses, and with K-9s have modified uniforms because of operational needs.

The advances of modern fabric design have created a plethora of uniform options for every climate and condition a bike patrol would work in. Some concepts are carried over from skiing, hiking, and mountain climbing, while others are borrowed from the experiences and equipment needs of triathletes and marathon runners. The result is custom uniforms that are far above the standard, or modified, patrol uniform in function and comfort, in most cases.

In considering the purchase of bike patrol uniforms one should first have a good understanding of the capabilities and function of various fabric types and their trade names. Some are for base layers next to the skin, while others are for in-between and outer layers, protecting you from the elements. Some fabrics have properties that cause a garment to be, for example, water proof or water repellent (for an outer layer), yet "breathable", so you won't overheat while wearing them. Base layers like CoolMax© and Drylete© are called "hydrophobic" fabrics and are designed to move moisture (perspiration) through the weave of the fabric away from the skin. CoolMax© transports, or "wicks", moisture to the outer surface of the garment where it will evaporate, and then channels cool air, as a result of the evaporative process, back through the fabric to cool the skin. On the other end of the woven spectrum, polyproylene and Thermstat© — both hydrophobic cold weather insulating materials — do basically the same thing with regard to transporting moisture as CoolMax©, but they prevent your body's warm air from escaping, thus maintaining that all important body core temperature while keeping you dry.

These are just two examples of the many materials that perform a wide variety of functions that make cycling, especially public safety cycling, more comfortable for the rider in all conditions. The only down-side of the "high-tech" custom uniforms is the additional cost over standard uniforms put to use for bike patrols. But the trade-off in this issue is rider comfort, which translates into how many, and how often, we can keep officers on the bike — if they're uncomfortable they won't want to ride, and shouldn't be required to in many circumstances, from a safety perspective. Climate extremes can have a profound, if not dangerous, effect on cyclists — sometimes before we realize the onset of the symptoms. Equipment that is designed not only for the riding position, but the cyclist's riding environment, will greatly enhance the ability, effectiveness, and safety of the public safety cyclist.

Care must also be taken not to stray too far from community expectations. During the 1970s, several

Fig. 3.3a. Proper summer uniform

Fig. 3.3b. Proper cold weather winter uniform

police departments, including the San Francisco Bay Area Transit Police, experimented with nontraditional uniforms, such as blazers and slacks. The thinking was that this "softened" the image of the police. But when called upon to do traditional tasks, such as directing traffic or arresting resistive suspects, people simply did not realize or believe that the officers were actually cops! The "uniforms" were quickly deemed impractical and abandoned.

Communities expect a certain "professional" appearance from their public safety personnel. For example, in the U.S., people have a mental image of national park rangers wearing a "Smokey the Bear hat," a gray shirt, small gold badge, and green jeans. The park service has cultivated this image for years, and it's hard to imagine a ranger dressed otherwise. Your uniform should communicate very clearly your official status. (Figs. 3.3a, 3.3b). Uniforms that are comfortable and meet the demands of policing on bikes are a must. So are uniforms that leave no question as to who is wearing them.

There are three places that your body touches the bicycle, your hands, feet and, last but most certainly not least, your butt. If you do not have the proper gear wrapped around these portions of your body, cycling for even a short period of time will feel like the torture. The following list of gear will help keep you on the road and out of bandages.

Helmets

The most obvious and necessary modification to the police uniform is a bicycle helmet. No single piece of equipment is more likely to save your life or reduce injury. Crashing is not a mere possibility when riding thousands of miles each year. Crashing is an inevitable, albeit unpleasant, experience which all bike officers eventually encounter. A correctly worn helmet dramatically increases the chances the officer will walk (or perhaps ride) away from an accident. A 1989 study, conducted by a Seattle emergency room, found that of the 99 cyclists it had treated that year for serious brain injury, only four had been wearing helmets at the time of their accident. The study concluded that an estimated 85 percent of severe head injuries to cyclists could be prevented by simply wearing a helmet.

There are many good-quality bicycle helmets on the market, in a wide variety of colors and styles. Finding one that compliments the uniform should not be a challenge. In terms of color, you must weigh visibility against tactical considerations. Some agencies use black helmets for tactical operations and light colored ones for regular patrol. A lycra helmet cover is an inexpensive way to do both. Helmet covers or decals are also easy ways to help identify unit members as law enforcement officers.

Another strong consideration for selecting a helmet is the number, size, and location of its air vents. The many helmets on the market today present a wide array of venting options, making it relatively easy to find one that suits your climate and riding environment. Don't underestimate the ability of the vent holes to keep your head in a comfortable temperature range. When you factor that we lose body heat through our heads faster than any other part of the body, it makes sense to cover it with the appropriate "heat exchange regulator" for existing conditions.

In warmer (hot) areas, a helmet with larger and more abundant vents is the way to go, especially one designed with "passive vents" along the lower front and side portions. The passive vents allow heat to escape without the aid of a moving air current, which is how the main vents are designed to work. As a lot of bike patrol work is done at very slow speeds, you can't take advantage of the breeze created by riding faster, so you need all the passive venting you can get. The more vents in a helmet, the better for warm or hot weather cycling.

In cooler or cold weather , the same physiological principle applies to loss of body heat, so smaller or no vents are preferable in these scenarios. This can be accomplished with a warm weather helmet by adding a

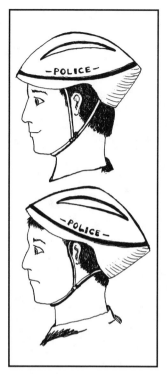

Fig. 3.3c. Demonstration of proper (top) and improper helmet fit (bottom)

Gore-Tex cover, or just taping the vents closed from the inside.

Any helmet you choose should be certified by either the American National Standards Institute (ANSI), the Snell Memorial Foundation, or the newer, American Standards Testing Materials (ASTM). The Consumer product Safety Commission (CPSC) is also considering bicycle helmet standards certification. Stickers inside the helmet identify which standards are met. The Snell standard is named after race car driver Pete Snell, who died in a car accident because of head injuries. These tests involve many things including primary and secondary impact capacities, and penetration tests. The latest ANSI standard at the time this was written is Z90.4. The best helmets have both ANSI (which is required by law) and the Snell Foundation stickers in them. Make this your minimum requirement.

The helmet should have a single triangulated nylon strap that lays in front and back of the ears. It's important that the strap be one piece and intertwined into the helmet shell from one side to the other. A strap that is attached to the helmet by any other means will fail to do its job correctly. The two-piece strap is likely to fail on impact if the helmet splits, because each half goes its separate way, leaving your skull to absorb the impact.

Make the helmet fit. The helmet should be worn level on the head. Wearing the helmet too far back on the head is the most common fitting mistake. The straps should be snug enough to keep the helmet from moving around on the head. The "Y" formed by the straps and buckles should be just below the ears. (Fig. 3.3c).

Not only does wearing a helmet make you a responsible rider, it sets an example for the general public.

**There are very few "nevers" in life, but here is one:
NEVER RIDE WITHOUT A HELMET!**

Eyewear

On a bike you have no windshield to keep dust, bugs, branches and other debris out of your eyes. Sunglasses help accomplish this, while simultaneously protecting your eyes from ultra violet rays. Amber lenses are great for sharpening up images in low light, fog, dawn, dusk, or overcast weather. Obviously, clear lenses are necessary for riding at night, but you should look to buy lenses that won't "bend" light causing distortion and glare, or the "star" effect, all of which could be hazardous at night. Invest in good quality eye protection; but before you hand over big bucks for the latest styles, make sure that your selection conforms to your agency's uniforms and equipment policy. Many manufacturers are offering substantial savings to police departments. Check with your local distributors and bike shops for a good deal.

Sounding Off

Chances are you won't have a siren on your bike and screaming isn't a good alternative. What's a bike cop to do? The answer for most cops is a whistle. However, the whistle must be readily accessible. Inexpensive lanyards, like the ones coaches use, and rubber mouth pieces are available at most sporting goods stores for around $1 each. The mouth piece will make things much easier on the teeth. There is a good reason why uniform ties are clip-ons, so don't wear the lanyard around the neck! Attach it to one of the velcro straps on your protective vest or an epaulet. Some officers modify the lanyard itself to make it a "brake away" style. If someone grabs and pulls, they get the whistle and not the cop. Or, you can opt for the more expensive electric cycle horn.

The Shirt

A regular wash and wear uniform shirt with some simple modifications, or shirts designed especially for bike patrol are excellent choices. The standard uniform shirt has a number of advantages over polo or golf shirts, which are popular in some areas. First, it looks virtually like those being work by other members of your agency. The epaulets can hold a radio mike and pockets hold penlights, writing utensils and other small items. Uniform and custom shirt construction is also superior to polo or golf shirts. This is an important feature in clothing that must be washed frequently.

The main concerns of the shirt design are: comfort in the riding position; the evaporation of perspiration; and the retention or expulsion of body heat. The riding position on a mountain bike requires the rider to have additional room in the back of shoulders, extra shirt tail length, etc., while still allowing for the wearing of a ballistic vest. The fabric will determine its breathability and moisture transport.

The increased movement of the bicycle officer can cause wear that a standard uniform shirt probably wasn't designed to cope with, but these are things that can usually be addressed in the design of a custom shirt. The most common problem for bike cops is the dislodging of the clutches that hold the badge and name tags to the breast of the shirt. Aside from reinforcing these areas, it is common and preferable to replace the metal badge and name plates with embroidered patches sewn to the shirt and jacket. This eliminates safety concerns of the officer being injured by a metal badge or pin during a crash or scuffle with a criminal. It also eliminates moving the items from inner to outer garments as the weather changes.

Another problem area is where the grip of a sidearm or the portable radio rubs against the sides of the shirt; without reinforcement it will eventually wear a hole through the fabric. If this modification is being considered for a standard uniform shirt, it might also be a good time to have mesh panels sewn into the sides of the shirt if more ventilation is desired.

Equipment Belts, Holsters, Etc.

Nylon web gear rigs are lighter and more comfortable during bike patrols than leather Sam Browne belts. Additionally, these set ups don't crack, warp, or shrink when they get wet. If your bike unit intends to be "all weather," this is the only way to go. Many departments now use security holsters, which are available in finishes that closely match the nylon. A word of caution concerning some security holsters. One bike officer discovered his holster swelled when exposed to rain, making it extremely secure until it dried out. Luckily, he discovered this at the range and not while confronting a felon.

Collapsing batons are another uniform option which seem to have been designed with bicycle officers in mind. But some officers have trouble getting these authorized and must carry a regular size baton. An effective way of coping with a full-size baton is to carry it in a collapsing baton holder. Some models allow the baton to be carried in a stable position. This overcomes the problem of the baton "flopping around." A few agencies have constructed very serviceable baton holders out of PVC pipe, which they mount on the rear rack of the bike. The down side of this method is that many departments train their officers to "exit the bike" (police-speak for "get off and drop the bike") when contacting suspects. If your baton is attached to the bike, it will be out of reach when you need it. By wearing the baton on the belt, it is always accessible and both hands are free as soon as you exit the bike.

There are some great little flashlights on the market now that can be worn on the belt, are rechargeable and put out as much light as their heavier cousins.

Shorts

Besides your bike helmet, nothing else so loudly proclaims "I am a bike cop!" as your shorts. Wearing long pants when working in 60+ degree weather puts uniformed riders at greater risk of heat-related health problems. These include chafing, heat stroke, and dehydration, not to mention a greater desire to seek out shade than crime. This can be overcome by simply wearing shorts.

There are several ways to go with uniform shorts. For the restricted budget (mainly newer units) it is possible to use cut-off uniform trousers worn over regular cycling shorts or similar briefs. The problem with this setup is that the cut-offs were not tailored to bend into the cyclist's position, so the back of the waistband will always want to pull down, causing the shirt to come untucked. Also, the "regular cut" of the trousers will bind in the crotch area because of the crouched riding position. Although they may be as close to the look of the regular uniform, they'll undoubtedly be very uncomfortable—especially with the addition of a padded short underneath—and they will stay wrinkled in the riding position when you stand off the bike.

Another option is to find a "coaches" or hiking type short which is made for athletic activity. This means there are breathable properties in the fabric and some elasticity, enabling it to return to its original shape when off the bike. These will generally wrinkle less than uniform cut-offs, but have a more casual look. Again, these can be worn with a cycling short or padded brief underneath.

If padded cycling shorts are worn under another short (this is advisable) the type of padding is important to your comfort. There are many types of padding ranging from real leather chamois, to cotton terry cloth. In addition, the seams of the pad come in different configurations, some of which can chafe when in repeated contact with sensitive skin areas. The most important aspect of any of them is how well it keeps your skin dry.

The combination of heat, moisture and friction produces blisters or, in cycling with the addition of bacteria, saddle sores. Saddle sores begin with hair follicles that become infected by bacteria and made worse by moisture, heat, and the lack of ventilation. All riding shorts should, at the very least, be rinsed with soap and water and dried after each use to prevent bacteria from forming. To get the best results use a mild detergent in cold water. Don't take any chances; buy good quality shorts or liners from a reputable cycle shop or manufacturer. You'll not soon forget a good case of saddle sores.

Finally, shorts made specifically for bike patrol, or bicycle touring, are the best alternative—money permitting. These shorts are constructed to allow the rider ample room in critical areas, as well as breathability in the fabric to keep the skin dry and free from chafing. They are usually available with either the padding sewn into the short or removable padding that can be taken out from the outer short for washing. In addition to making them to each officer's measurements, many of the manufacturers of bike patrol specific equipment will modify the shorts to special needs. For example, you may want a special positioning of the belt loops to accommodate a certain gun belt, or maybe an extra pocket sewn in to hold a can of O.C. spray.

Agencies in warmer climates can expect that once the tradition of long pants has been broken by bike officers, regular patrol officers will want to know, "How come we can't be comfortable?" Well, why not? One bike qualified officer who primarily worked a car beat, sustained poison oak over both his legs after crashing in an off-duty mountain bike race. Rather than take off sick because of his inability to wear long pants, he asked for and was granted permission to wear his uniform shorts on regular patrol. Citizens thought it was great!

Hand Protection

The hands need protection in the form of cycling gloves both from abrasions suffered in falls, and to help prevent Carpal Tunnel Syndrome. You can find these in black and other non-day-glow colors. When selecting gloves be sure that they are not so thick that they alter your grip on the handlebars. Gloves that are too thick will cause you to grip the bars more firmly in an effort to gain control. The extra padding in effect makes the grips thicker and less of your hand and fingers fit around it, so you squeeze tighter, causing hand fatigue to set in more quickly.

In cold weather, a full-finger glove that does not inhibit writing or shooting is a must. You will not be able to remove any cycling glove fast enough in a shooting situation, so be sure you practice shooting while wearing them. It's important that you understand what they do to your grip.

Footwear

Plain athletic shoes are okay for those who ride occasionally, but full-time bike patrol officers need a good mountain bike shoe to prevent painful foot conditions. Mountain bike shoes have stiff soles, which help protect the foot against the mountain bike pedal cages that have sharp teeth for a positive grip.

Any extended riding (and 8 hours a day is well beyond "extended") can cause plenty of foot problems. A medical condition that can arise from using running shoes while cycling is called "Morton's Neuroma." This is a condition where the small bones and connective tissues of the feet are damaged because of improper support of the foot while on the pedals.

A cross trainer looks much like any gym shoe except that it has a fairly stiff sole. It effectively spreads the very small pedal bearing surface over the area of the whole foot. Despite their stiffness, cross trainers are easy to walk or run in.

Mountain bike or touring shoes are stiffer than cross trainers and most offer the option of mounting recessed cleats for a particular pedal retention system. These shoes are the best hedge against foot discomfort brought on by long hours of riding, but they do have a drawback as they relate to police cycling: they can be difficult to run in due to the inflexibility of the soles—at least until they're broken in. Before buying these type of shoes, walk around the store in them to experience the stiffness and then make your decision.

Mountain bike or "off-road" shoes have stiff soles for pedaling comfort and "aggressive" sole patterns to enhance traction off the bike. These shoes are designed to accommodate the types of cleats used in pedal retention systems commonly used on mountain bikes, whereas touring shoes are not, and have a smoother sole pattern. Cleated retention pedals will increase the efficiency with which you deliver power to the pedals and can aid in control of the bike. These systems require a lot of practice to get used to having your feet, literally, "attached " to the pedals. You must be extremely proficient before attempting to employ them for patrol work.

Should you choose to use off-road shoes and a cleated pedal retention system you'll notice these type of shoes have the mountings for the cleats recessed into the sole below the tread knobs: this is to protect the cleat from damage and to allow you to walk on the sole of the shoe without the cleat protruding below it (as is the case with a lot of road bike shoes). The only drawback, aside from the rider having to quickly obtain the skill of clipping the shoe in and out of the pedal, is that when the sole wears down from walking, the metal cleats begin to make contact with the ground. This can be slippery to walk in, especially on hard surfaces. Check the sole depth frequently to avoid ice skating when you'd rather be walking or running.

A good choice for winter and inclement weather are the waterproof, lace-up "police boots," which come with many lining options, such as Gore-Tex© or CoolMax©, and have good soles for cycling. Just be sure they'll fit inside the toe-clips and straps of your pedals, as they're generally wider than the shoes pedal manufacturers had in mind.

Most of the mountain bike or touring shoes, and even some cross trainers, will not conform to some agency uniform guidelines due to their color or prominent logos. Many officers have found that these shoes can be dyed black (or what ever color is appropriate) with good results. It pays to have someone who is experienced in dying leather or synthetics tackle the job though.

Another debate is the subject of socks. How high? What color? Logo? Stripes? Cyclists wear ankle high socks for a good reason: chain grease. Don't spend the money for knee high athletic socks with "police" embroidered on them, only to ruin them with chain grease. White socks are inexpensive, easy to find and look most appropriate with cycling-style shoes. Dark socks may achieve a better appearance with long pant uniforms worn in cold conditions. There is no health advantage to wearing white, so it comes down to preference. However, choose socks made of material that will move the moisture created by perspiration away from your skin to prevent blisters.

Protective Vests

If your climate allows, wear a protective vest. Vented shirts and T-shirts made out of perspiration wicking materials, such as Cool-Max©, can help increase your comfort. For bike officers, the vest also provides another layer of material between you and the road. A welcome barrier for that inevitable trip to the pavement.

Winter Clothing

Foul weather uniforms designed especially for bike patrols are now manufactured by a number of companies. These uniforms are available in a wide variety of colors. They are also so superior to the ones currently being used by patrol officers that many departments are embracing them for mainstream patrol use. As an increasing number of departments recognize the benefits of these "high tech" garments, this trend will no doubt continue.

Clothing selection in the winter months is very crucial. If you make a bad choice, you run the risk of officers not riding because of foul weather conditions. Or, worse yet, you risk the possibility of officers injuring themselves because of the cold. Not seeing bike officers out every day leads the public to believe that bicycle patrols are only effective during fair weather. In the Midwest, winters mean extreme cold and snow. Yet, many bike units continue to ride throughout the winter. This is because of proper clothing selection and dedication.

Layering

The key to dressing for winter riding is in layering. Layering creates "micro-climates" between each garment, which serves as a barrier to the cold more effectively than a single garment, no matter how thick.

Generally, layering consists of two or more layers of clothing, each with a different purpose. By layering with several thin garments you retain body heat and permit more body movement than with heavier clothing.

The first is the base layer. Fabrics used for this layer are made of the hydrophobic materials that you want next to your bare skin to absorb and get rid of moisture. This layer includes the undershirt, underpants, "long Johns", socks, ear warmers, balaclavas, glove liners, full face hoods, and anything that will be against bare skin. That includes ballistic vest carriers as well. (Some companies are producing CoolMax© vest carriers that work well alone, or with an insulating layer.) Cotton is not a good base layer because it stays wet, but wool and the man-made hydrophobic materials work well to wick moisture.

The second layer can be either an insulating or outer (wind) shell. The insulating layer helps keep your body heat in while allowing moisture to evaporate. Wool works well as an insulator because it maintains heat while wet, but other materials such as fleece, Wicktec©, and Fieldsensor© are better in most cases. Again, cotton does a poor job of evaporating moisture well enough to depend on it as an insulating layer, so look for these other fabrics to form your layers.

The outer layer will deter, or stop, wind, rain or snow from penetrating the inner layer, and some will allow moisture to evaporate from inside. Outer layer fabrics can be wind proof, water proof, and water resistant, yet still allow moisture to escape from the inside out. Examples of these are: Supplex©; GoreTex©; and Solar Alpha©.

When using a three layer group you have the option of removing one of the outer two layers to adjust to the climate and the enormous body heat you'll generate while pedaling. And, as the garments are designed to be thin, they should store easily on the bike until needed again.

With any number of garments used in layering a good adage to remember is: "If you feel warm and comfortable when you begin your ride, you're probably dressed too warm for cycling." You should feel a bit on the chilly side when you set out; your "engine" will generate enough heat soon enough.

Long-Sleeved Shirts. As a cycling shirt, the standard issue long-sleeved shirt is worse than its short-sleeved counterpart. It too needs more room in the shoulders, but it also constricts the arms around the elbows and forearms restricting movement and possibly cutting off blood circulation. Winter riding is a good reason to find an alternate to this shirt.

The standard long-sleeved winter uniform shirt comes in various fabric blends, with the wool blends serving as a better insulating layer than the polyester blends. Wool blends are still not the best fabric for allowing total evaporation or transport of moisture, however. If the ride will be cold enough to require the use of a jacket as an outer layer, try wearing a wool or fleece sweater underneath as your insulator. Some departments approve and issue wool "commando" type sweaters in the winter months for this purpose instead of the uniform shirt. If you can't replace the shirt, be sure you're wearing a good base layer that will keep your skin dry and warm.

Jackets. It is important for the outer shell to shelter you from the elements and to allow freedom of movement. The material and its liner are equally important. The liner should act as a moisture barrier (water proof) to keep the garment from sticking to your skin when worn as a second layer shell. Other features of the jacket should include: a two-way zipper; wrist closures; a hook and loop closure on the collar to keep it from flapping in the wind and to allow adjustment of the opening for ventilation; and a ventilation flap on the back, just below the shoulder blades.

A winter jacket should be cut long enough in the back (or have a way to fix it to your belt) to keep it from riding up past your waistband and allowing cold air in. Likewise, the collar should fold up high enough to cover the back of the neck up to the bottom of the helmet. Many manufacturers also make jackets that have zippered arms that can be removed to form a vest or bolero, this is a very useful feature when the temperature is not quite cold enough to warrant the full jacket.

Remember that you must wear a gun belt and be able to reach any of its accessories while wearing the jacket. When choosing a jacket find out how the gun belt will stay in place if worn over the jacket: Will it have loops; hook and loop fasteners? If worn underneath your jacket, is access to your weapon and radio adequate? Do you need pockets, a microphone loop, or reflective materials?

Pants. When the weather drops below 60 degrees, you should have something over your legs because of the body's inability to maintain warmth in the knees. The knee is especially susceptible to injuries from the cold because its tendons and ligaments are only insulated by a few millimeters of skin; whereas other joints have the added protection of larger muscles and body fat.

In climates where temperatures never really get cold enough to wear winter riding pants, but it's cool enough to need protection for the knees, a light riding pant worn over light-weight polypropylene, ThermaStat© "leg warmers," or tights will do just fine. If you use the leg warmers, you will need to wear a cycling short underneath to hold the tops of them to keep them from rolling down. The light-pant/leg-warmer combination is more versatile than one pair of winter weight pants, because: 1) the leg warmers usually can be removed without removing outer pants (equipped with zippers at the ankle/calf); and, 2) the light pants worn without the leg warmers are less cumbersome than winter riding pants.

The optimum type of cold weather cycling pants are made by companies that specialize in uniforms for bicycle patrol. Because these pants have become so highly evolved, it's just a matter of looking at several products and making a decision. Skimping with cold weather gear will severely reduce the effectiveness of your patrol unit.

Winter Gloves and Hats. Winter gloves and balaclavas are an absolute must for riding in extreme cold weather. When selecting gloves, look for the thinnest ones that will keep you warm and still allow good control of the bike. And above all, be sure you can draw and fire your weapon accurately while wearing them.

The balaclava keeps heat from escaping from your neck and head which is essential to cold weather survival, since these are the areas you lose body heat from most. Since the balaclava is a base layer garment, look for those made of hydrophobic materials.

CONCLUSION

It is essential to the success of a bicycle patrol that the proper clothing, bicycles and equipment be utilized. If these essential items are not of a good quality, a bicycle patrol officer can suffer in many ways—from being too cold or too hot to their bicycle breaking down in the middle of a chase.

CHAPTER FOUR:
BICYCLE MAINTENANCE

Very few public safety officers do any maintenance on their patrol cars, motorcycles, ambulances, or emergency vehicles. Yet, bike-mounted public safety officers will perform maintenance on their "vehicle" on a routine basis. For that reason it becomes extremely important to know the basics of bicycle maintenance. Some things need to be done daily, some weekly, and others monthly or annually. Much of this depends on the riding conditions, but also on the rider.

4.1 BEGIN AT THE BASICS: ABC QUICK CHECK

One of the fundamentals of maintenance is what is commonly called the ABC Quick Check. This is done before each shift for your safety, as well as the safety of others.

"A" is for air. Take a few moments to check your tire pressure. Most tires will do best at 50-55 PSI. Initially, you may need to use a gauge, but after you've felt the tire several times, you'll be able to check by hand. (Fig. 4.1a). While doing so, you should also look for damage to the sidewalls and tread. Damage to the sidewall is common if the brakes are not adjusted properly. If the bands are showing below the surface, the tire needs immediate replacing. If this is noticed in the field, or if a flat is caused by a sidewall tear, use a folded dollar bill between the sidewall and the tube for a temporary fix.

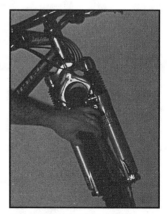

Fig. 4.1a. Feeling for air pressure as part of the ABC Quick Check

Fig. 4.1b. As part of step "B," make sure to check for proper brake pad alignment

Fig. 4.1c. As part of step "C," check for play in the bottom bracket and crankarms

Fig. 4.1d. As part of the "Quick" step, check for proper quick release spoon placement

"B" is for brakes. This is extremely important if your agency uses "pool" bikes, which are those shared by more than one rider. The last thing you want to happen is to get your bicycle up to 30 mph downhill, have a light turn red, to find you have only front brakes. Yes, they are the more effective brakes, but will you stop in time without going over the handlebars? To check the brakes, simply hold the brake lever down and roll the bike forward and back. Visually inspect the brake pads for proper wear. (Fig. 4.1b). Check the cables and housings, making sure the cables travel smoothly and the ends of the cable are not frayed. If the cables stick, place lubrication at the ends of the housings, then work it in by applying the brakes several times. Frayed cables should be replaced.

"C" is for crank. The power train of the bicycle, the crank set consists of the bottom bracket, the crankarms and chainrings. Problems with the crank set have been minimized over the last couple of years with sealed bottom brackets now being the rule, rather than the exception. To check the crank set, take the left and right crankarms in your hands and attempt to move them sideways. (Fig. 4.1c). If both move, you've got a problem with your bottom bracket. If only one moves, then the individual crankarm is most likely loose and must be secured. Never ride a bike with a loose crankarm. It will further loosen the crankarm, which could fall off.

"Quick" is for the quick releases on your hubs. The primary point to remember here is "tight, but not too tight." If the quick release is too tight, the bearings in the wheel may be compressed causing damage. The proper pressure is obtained by pushing on the lever so that it leaves an impression on the palm of your hand. You should also remember to keep closed levers facing up and back to minimize the chances of them catching on anything while you ride. (Fig. 4.1d).

"Check" is for check to see that your derailleurs and shift levers are working properly. Take a brief, slow ride before starting out to check both components. Following the ABC Quick Check, you are ready to start your shift.

4.2 Rules of Maintenance

B efore beginning any bicycle repairs, the three basic rules of maintenance must be addressed.

RULE #1: Make sure the right tools are on hand. Pliers and vice grips are not the right tools to use when tightening your headset. A crescent wrench for the most part is not the right tool for bicycle repairs either. A number of key components on your bicycle may be aluminum and are easily stripped. You'll want to ensure the tools you use are snug, and have as much surface-to- surface contact as possible. If your unit intends to do the majority of its own repairs, here is a list of the tools you are likely to need:

Basic Bike Tool Kit:

- 3, 4, 5, & 6mm allen wrenches
- 8-10mm brake wrenches
- Spare tube, patch kit and pump
- Tire lever
- Spoke wrench

General Tools For Minor Maintenance:

- Headset wrenches
- Complete set of allen wrenches, SAE & Metric
- Crank bolt wrench
- Complete set of metric box-end wrenches, 5mm-17mm
- Complete set of screwdrivers
- Adjustable wrenches (small, medium and large)
- Floor pump with gauge
- Pedal wrench
- Freewheel and cassette remover
- Chain rivet tool
- Tire patching equipment
- Chain lube
- Brake wrenches

Basic Tools Needed To Do Department Maintenance:

(In addition the those previously mentioned)

- Repair stand
- Axle cone wrenches, 13 -16mm
- Third or fourth hand brake tool
- Tire lever
- Truing stand, and spoke wrench set
- Crank extractor
- Measuring calipers
- Bottom bracket wrench set
- "Y" socket wrench cutters
- 8, 9, & 10mm cable and housing
- Chain lube & axle grease
- Apron & rags
- Brushes, solvent, & containers

RULE #2: **Always check the basics before going any further.** There are people who have "trued" their wheel when all that was needed was to realign it with the bicycle and tighten the quick release. This mistake is not only embarrassing, it's labor intensive.

RULE #3: **Never try fixing something you do not understand.** You will almost always do more damage than repair.

You may find it's more cost-effective for your department to pay an experienced bicycle mechanic to do some repairs. (How to find a good mechanic is addressed later in this chapter.) In other cases, you may want to "save" money by letting officers work on the bicycles during down time. By following the three rules of maintenance, you'll know when to take the bicycle into the shop, rather than attempting the repair yourself.

4.3 GENERAL MAINTENANCE

Flat Tires

The most common repair is fixing a flat tire. Everybody dreads having to fix a flat, but with practice (and the right equipment) it can be done in 5-10 minutes with minimal difficulty. Whether front or rear tire, the wheel must be removed from the bicycle. To do so, release the brakes and the quick release mechanism. Most bicycles have small ridges at the base of the front forks. These help hold the wheel on the bicycle but require the quick release to be fairly loose before you can pull them away from the bicycle. In the case of the rear wheel, it is best to shift the bicycle's gears onto the small freewheel cog before removing the wheel. This allows less chain tension and makes removal and replacement of the wheel easier.

Once the wheel has been removed, visually inspect the tire for whatever caused the flat. If you are able to locate an object, mark its location and remove it. This will make finding the hole in the tube easier. If nothing is located visually, check the surface by feel, using a sock, rag or cycling glove. Under no circumstances should you use your bare hand. Whatever caused the flat can just as easily slice your hand.

Fig. 4.3a. Inserting tire lever into tire bead while making sure the valve stem is at the bottom

The next step is to remove the tire from the rim. A plastic tire iron or other special tool designed for this purpose works well. Don't use screwdrivers, butter knives, or other metal objects. You will only add to your problems. Start with the side opposite the valve stem. (Fig. 4.3a). Any damage to the valve stem is non-repairable, so this area is always "last out and first in." When the tire has been separated from the rim on one side, you may remove the inner tube, remembering the "last out and first in" rule with the valve stem. Visually inspect the inside of the tire for whatever caused the flat. If you are dealing with a new bicycle and it's

A DIFFERENT KIND OF MAINTAINANCE: YOUR BODY
BASIC INFORMATION ON NUTRITION

Any cop can tell you—but a bicycle cop will tell you quicker—eating right is an essential part of fitness. Nutrition is as personal as it is important. Any trip to your local bookstore will allow you to discover some of the volumes of information that have been written on nutrition so you can tailor your eating to your lifestyle. Below is simple information from which to build your knowledge-bank on nutrition.

Eat food high in carbohydrates: Seventy percent of your daily caloric intake should come from carbohydrates. Carbohydrates are simply the most important fuel for working muscles. They are the most efficient and quickly available source of energy your body has. Carbohydrates convert to glucose, which is a simple sugar in your body's complex make-up that translates into energy. One gram of carbohydrate is equivalent to four calories. Common carbohydrates include fruits, vegetables, grains, beans, lentils, rice, and pasta.

Avoid fat: Only 15% of your daily caloric intake should come from fat. Fat does play an important role in the balanced diet, however, too much is bad. Fat has twice the calories per unit of weight than carbohydrates or protein and is a less efficient energy source than carbohydrates. Fat robs you of needed energy—the body will use all of its energy to digest the fatty food rather than allow the energy to be used by your muscles to propel your bike. In any given food, there should not be more than 30% of the calories derived from fat. You can figure this percentage by multiplying the amount of fat grams by nine: each fat gram has nine calories. If a candy bar has 12 grams of fat, and you multiply 12 x 9, that means that 108 of the candy bar's 200 calories are from fat. Divide 108 by 200 and you get the percentage of fat in that candy bar: 54% That is way over 30%! Common fats include margarine, butter, cooking oil, cream cheese, dairy products, animal fats in meat, and "hidden" fats in commercial foods.

Protein: Twelve percent of your daily diet should be derived from protein. Protein is a necessary component in rebuilding muscle, and has so many other important jobs that it is rarely used by our body as a fuel source. It only gets significantly tapped as a fuel source as you get closer and closer to running out of carbohydrate muscle fuel. Common sources of low-fat protein include lean meats, low-fat or non-fat dairy products, egg whites, and a proper combination of fruits, vegetables, legumes and grains.

Watch your sweet tooth: Three percent of your daily caloric intake should come from sugar. Did you know all the sugar your body needs can be obtained by fruit? Yet the average American will consume more than 25 pounds of refined sugar a year. Sugar, when not utilized in the bloodstream during exercise, will be deposited in your fatty tissue, causing it to increase.

Drink plenty of water: See the side-bar on page 70 for more information on the importance of H_2O.

Fig. 4.3b. Rim tape has shifted, exposing the spoke nipple; this is the cause of many flats

Fig. 4.3c. Roughing the tube

your first flat, check the inside of the rim for any spots that are very rough or pointed. Also, make certain that rim tape adequately covers the spoke nipple holes. (Fig. 4.3b). Under pressure, tubes will try to force their way into any space, no matter how small. It is not uncommon to find rough spots on new rims; they are easy to grind down with a light file.

You are now ready to find the hole in the tube. Usually the hole can be heard and felt once the tube has been filled with air. If not, a little water from your water bottle or saliva should work. Slow leaks can be very difficult to find in the field, and may require immersing the tube to find the leak. When you find the hole, circle it, taking care not to puncture the tire again! Make sure the surface is dry. Then, using a small piece of sandpaper, rough the area in all directions. (Fig. 4.3c).

Apply a fair quantity of glue from your patch kit to an area slightly larger than the patch. (Fig. 4.3d). The glue must dry to the point of being sticky before the patch can be applied. Blow on it to speed up the process. Once the glue is dry, place the patch on the glue and apply pressure. (Fig. 4.3e). Place some additional glue around the edge of the patch and allow it to dry. Do NOT "test" the patch by inflating the tube outside the tire. It will not hold. The patch needs the resistance of the tire for the patch to hold.

You are now ready to place the tube back into the tire. It works best to put just enough air in the tube to make it round. Next, place the valve stem back into the rim. Put the tube in the tire, then put the tire back on the rim. This process requires more finesse than force. (Fig. 4.3f). Be careful not to pinch the tube against the rim, or you will be back to square one. Before putting additional air into the tube, make sure none of it is exposed between the tire and the rim.

As this point, make sure that the valve stem is straight. If it isn't, just strike the tire in the same direction the tube needs to go. This will cause both the tire and the tube to spin—as long as you don't have more than 10-15 PSI in the tube—and your valve stem will be straightened.

Remember, it does you absolutely no good to repair a flat if you do not have a source of air. Use either a bicycle pump or compressed air canister. Do not use a gas station pump unless you take care to inflate it gradually. This type of pump will inflate much faster than a hand or floor pump. Stop and check every couple of seconds to make sure that the tube is not being pinched between the tire and the rim, and that the bead of the tire is properly seated in the rim.

If you have Presta valves instead of Schrader valves, make sure you have the correct adapter. (Fig. 4.3g).

Once you have fully inflated the tube, place the wheel back on the bicycle. Remember to center the wheel and secure it with the quick releases. Reattach the brakes and do another ABC Quick Check.

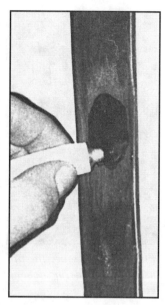

Fig. 4.3d. Applying the glue to an area slightly larger than the patch

Brakes

Of all the components on your bicycle, the most essential for safety reasons are the brakes. Without derailleurs you can't get moving very fast, but you won't get hurt. Having no brakes is a different story. When the bicycle is new, everything should be adjusted properly. As time goes by and the bicycle gets used, things begin to change. Cables stretch. Pads wear. Rims may go out of true or develop flat spots. All these things influence the effectiveness of the brakes and may require adjustment.

Cable stretch and pad wear are simple fixes. There are barrel adjustments just beyond the brake levers on the cable path. (Fig. 4.3h). By turning these out from the brake levers, you'll be decreasing the distance the cable must travel, therefore, closing the brake pads closer to the rim. When doing this, check the pads to make sure they are wearing properly. If the pad is hitting periodically on the rotating tire, you are likely developing a flat spot on the rim and the pad must be ad-

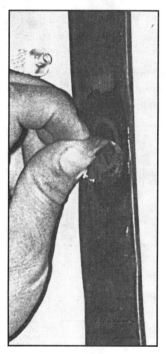

Fig. 4.3e. Peeling clear backing from applied patch

Fig. 4.3f. Resecure the tire using your hands and nothing else

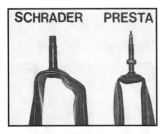

Fig.4.3g. Valves come in two types, Presta and Schrader

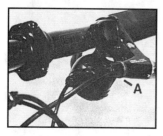

Fig. 4.3h. "A" points to the barrel adjustment for the front brake

justed down. Whenever adjusting the pad, remember to "toe in" the pad (which means that the forward end of the pads should hit the rim first when the brakes are applied). This will allow for full pad use as the forward energy of the wheel slightly rotates the pad forward. (Fig. 4.3i). The difference between the front and rear of the pad relative to the rim should be about 1/16th of an inch— about the thickness of a dime, which you can use to measure the distance. Chirping or squealing brakes are almost always a result of improperly toed pads. The problem is simple to fix, and ensures not only better braking, but stealthier and thus safer approaches to suspects!

In the event you need to replace a cable, remember these three things: 1) Turn the barrel adjuster at the lever out about 1 1/2 turns at set-up, this allows some room to turn it back in (increasing the distance between the brake blocks and the rim) should a wheel go slightly out of true and the brakes rub the rim at the bend. This is handy because you can make the adjustment while on the road and true the wheel later. Don't wait too long though, because the wheel will gradually get worse and eventually "taco," or fail; 2) While replacing a cable, take the opportunity to inspect the housing for damage (and rough edges on its ends) and lubricate if needed. 3) Never cut the cable until after it is in place and then only with the right tool (the use of special cable cutters prevents the strands at the end of the cable from unraveling.) Cables should be cut with approximately 2 inches extra. It is suggested that only one cable be replaced at a time. This way the correct cable path will be obvious.

There is one other adjustment mechanism for the brakes that should be discussed. A tension adjustment screw located on the non-quick release caliper (left front/ right rear) will fine tune the tension. (Fig. 4.3j). If one caliper is closing quicker than the other, this screw will correct it. Turning the screw inward will increase the caliper tension on that side and releasing it outward will decrease caliper tension.

Derailleurs

The primary adjustment mechanisms for both the front and rear derailleurs are barrel adjustments. The adjustment for the front derailleur is near the shifter on the cable path. (Fig. 4.3k). The rear derailleur has one at both ends of the cable path. (Figs. 4.3l, 4.3m). These barrel adjustments will handle 90 percent of the necessary adjustments. The two screws located on the top of the front derailleur and back of the rear derailleur are maximum in and out settings that prevent the derailleurs from moving the chain past the first and last rear cogs, and off either side of the front chainrings. They were set when the bike was assembled, and are used only for limiting the inward and outward movement of the derailleurs. (Figs. 4.3n, 4.3o). They have no function in adjusting how the derailleurs shift from cog-to-cog or chainring-to-chainring. The next alternative is a cable adjustment.

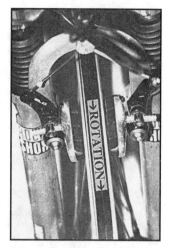

Fig. 4.3i. Proper "toe in" of the brake pads

Fig. 4.3j. Adjusting the brake tension adjustment screw

Whenever doing a cable adjustment, you must remember to back off the barrel adjustments—again, so that this adjustment mechanism will be available again later. Once completely backed off, turn them each two turns. This will give you an easy adjustment mechanism should you over tighten the cable. To adjust the rear derailleur shift the chain onto the smallest cog in the rear and the middle chainring in front. Loosen the lock nut that attaches the cable to the rear derailleur. Next, pull the cable through the locking plate under that nut until there is no slack in it, and tighten the lock nut. Re-check the cable for slack where it is exposed from the housing—usually along the chain-stay or seat-stay of the frame, and re-tighten as necessary. It should not be slack, but not 'piano wire' taught either.

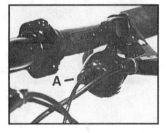

Fig. 4.3k. "A" points to the front derailleur barrel adjustment

Hopefully you'll be working with a repair stand, but if not, have someone lift the rear wheel off the ground while you turn the pedals and shift through the gears to check for any needed adjustments. Before making any adjustments, look to see what kind of movement is tak-

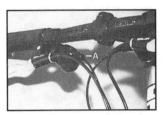

Fig. 4.3l. "A" points out the rear derailleur barrel adjustment located at the shifter

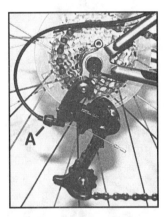

Fig. 4.3m. "A" points out the rear derailleur barrel adjustment

Fig. 4.3n. Front derailleur: A - limit screws; B - cable attachment clamp nut

ing place. If the chain is rubbing on the outside of the front derailleur cage, you need to increase cable tension. If the chain is rubbing on the inside of the front derailleur cage, you need to slightly decrease cable tension. Remember, the larger the chain ring, the more cable tension that is necessary.

By watching the chain movement on the rear freewheel you'll be able to see whether it is moving up or down (that is, whether the chain is attempting to slide into a higher or lower gear). The chain attempting to move onto a larger freewheel cog indicates too much cable tension. The chain attempting to drop down onto a smaller freewheel cog indicates not enough cable tension. Fine tune the chain movement with the barrel adjusters; usually no more than 1/4 turn in either direction is needed. If adjustments don't seem to be curing the shifting problems check for the following:

- Bent derailleur cage
- Bent drop-out (the part of the frame that the derailleur is bolted to)
- Stretched chain

With the exception of the stretched chain, you should have an experienced bike mechanic check/repair these maladies.

With the advent of grip shifters, these minor adjustments are easily done while riding. The barrel adjustments are larger and more easily accessible. Additionally, you can see on your hand shifting mechanism which gear you should be in.

Derailleur Cage Damage

Another problem you may encounter is damage to the cage of either the front or rear derailleur. The best way to avoid the problem, at least with the rear derailleur, is to get a rear derailleur guard. (Another way to avoid rear derailleur damage is to drop the bike only on the left side, away from the derailleur.) Rear derailleur guards are inexpensive compared to the cost of repairing or replacing a derailleur. If you do manage to break a derailleur, do not attempt to fix it yourself. An experienced mechanic has a much better chance of saving the derailleur.

Chain Break & Repair

There are three situations that would require the use of a chain breaking tool:

- Your chain becomes twisted or jammed.
- Your chain breaks apart while riding.
- Your chain is worn and in need of replacement.

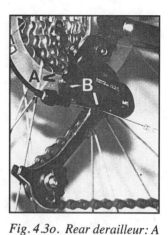

Fig. 4.3o. Rear derailleur: A - limit screws; B - cable attachment clamp nut

You can check the chain's wear by holding a ruler next to the outside plates. Start the ruler on one of the pins that goes through the plates and follow along to the 12-inch mark. (Fig. 4.3p). That mark should line up with another pin. If the pin is past the mark by more than 1/8 inch, it's probably time to think about replacing it. The price of a chain is far less than replacing the chainrings or rear cogs it will cause to wear prematurely. A nifty alternative to the ruler method is Park Tool's Chain Checker tool.

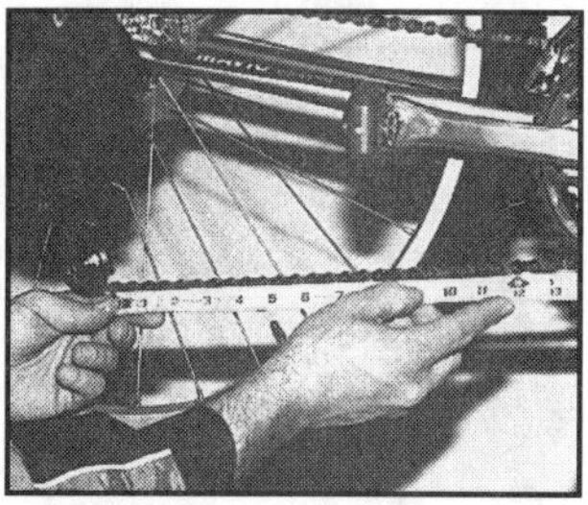

Fig. 4.3p. Using a tape measure to check a chain for wear

If any of the above occur, you must use your chain tool to break apart the chain using the following steps:

Shift the chain to the smallest freewheel cog and the smallest chainring to ease the derailleur spring tension on the chain, which will make it easier to work with. A handy homemade tool that helps make this job a little easier can be made from a wire coat hanger and will fit nicely in any bag. Take a 6-inch piece of coat hanger and bend the ends into "Ls" about 1-inch long. Pull the chain together to make a loop hang down and insert the ends of the wire tool into the chain from above, allowing the loop to exist without derailleur spring tension. Now you can work on the looped section with your chain breaker without the spring tension. (Fig. 4.3q).

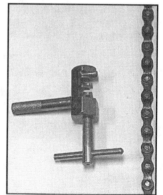

Fig. 4.3q. Chain tool ready for use

Next, shift the chain across the inside of the outermost wall of the chain tool, lining up one of the chain pins with the pin on the chain tool. Slowly and steadily

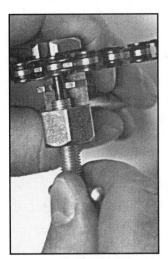

Fig. 4.3r. Pushing the chain pin slowly with chain tool

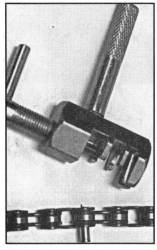

Fig. 4.3s. Chain pin pushed out, ready for disassembly

turn the handle of the chain tool clockwise, spiraling the pin of the tool and pushing the pin of the chain out through the side of the chain link. (Fig. 4.3r). DO NOT remove the pin from the chain completely. Push the pin outward until the end of the pin is even with the outer most point of the chain tool. (Fig. 4.3s). Then, turning the handle of the tool counter clockwise, back the pin of the tool out of the chain link. Your chain can then be pulled apart with light twisting force. (Fig. 4.3t). Reassemble the chain using these steps in reverse.

4.4 OTHER MAINTENANCE ISSUES

Headsets and Bottom Brackets

Two common problems easily solved are loose head sets and bottom brackets. These can be checked with minimal effort. The headset check is done by applying the front brakes then rocking the bicycle forward and back. The looseness is indicated by movement at the top of the head tube. There are two nuts at the top of the headtube. Both apply themselves to the forks. The lower one, which is slightly larger, holds the upper headset bearings in place. The upper one acts as a locking nut which prevents the lower one from loosening. (Fig. 4.4a). If either of these have become loose, you feel movement while doing the headset check. If no tools are available, just tighten them with your hands — but remember that you will have to repeat this every half hour, or until you get to the proper tools. The common sizes of these nuts are either 32mm or 36mm. You'll need two wrenches to properly tighten the headset. (Fig. 4.4b). Begin by tightening the lower nut down until the movement in the headset is eliminated. Check to make sure the bicycle still steers easily and smoothly. If not, you may have over-tightened the nut. Once you have set the nut at the proper tightness, tighten it one quarter turn more. Next, tighten the upper nut down onto the lower nut. The final step is to turn the lower nut into the upper nut, holding it into place. By then backing off the lower nut into the upper one, you have locked them into place and added just enough play to allow free movement of the bearings. A little play reduces the pressure on the ballbearing. on the race. Too much pressure will cause premature wear called "Brinelling."

If you have an "Ahead©" brand set, rather than a traditional headset, the process is even more simple. (Fig. 4.4c). Simply tighten the Allen nut located on top of the step at the pivot point. (Fig. 4.4d). A few bicycle manufacturers are choosing to use the Ahead© set.

Adjusting the bottom bracket is no more difficult. The bottom bracket check is done as part of the ABC Quick Check. By taking control of both the crankarms and attempting to move them sideways, you will be able to detect any looseness. Pay attention to what is actually moving. If only one side is moving, the answer is simple: tighten the crankarm on that side using either an appropriate size Allen or a crank-bolt wrench, depending on what style of fixing bolt you have. If both sides of the crank are moving, you will need to check the bottom bracket itself.

A sealed bottom bracket may have loose cups. The cups are what hold the bottom bracket into the frame. You'll need to remove the crankarms in order to secure the cups. A special tool is needed to install, remove or adjust these threaded cups. If the problem returns, a fixing, bolt-securing product such as Loctite© is suggested. If securing these cups does not fix the problem, the sealed bottom bracket needs replacing (or, if the cups are plastic/nylon, replace with metal ones). This is done by removing the crankarms, releasing the cups, and then pulling out the bottom bracket. (Fig. 4.4e). The new bottom bracket is then installed. Both cups are secured, while still maintaining smooth axle movement. The

Fig. 4.3t. Inner and outer portions of a chain link

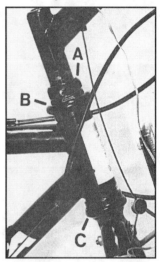

Fig. 4.4a. The standard headset: A - locknut; B - adjustable bearing cup; C - fixed lower bearing cup

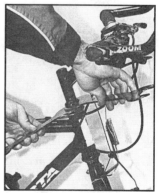

Fig. 4.4b. Headset wrenches being used

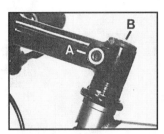

Fig. 4.4c. The Ahead© set: A - stem clamp Allen bolt; B - bearing adjustment Allen bolt

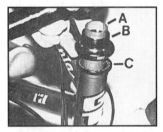

Fig. 4.4d. A - threadless steering tube; B - spacer rings; C - upper Ahead© set bearings

Fig. 4.4e. Sealed bottom bracket on left, bottom bracket tool on right

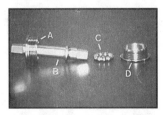

Fig. 4.4f. Adjustable bottom bracket: A - fixed bearing cup; B - spindle; C - bearings; D - adjustable bearing cup and lockring

crankarms are then put back (remember to place the chain on the small chainring to make your initial shifting easier).

If your bicycle does not have a sealed bottom bracket, you will need to adjust the play via two large nuts on the non-chainring side of the bottom bracket. (Fig. 4.4f). This can be done without removing the crankarms by using a bottom bracket wrench. As with the headset nuts, you must be careful not to over tighten. If this does not solve the problem, you will need to open up the bottom bracket.

First remove the chain from the chainring and gently lay it on top of the bottom bracket housing or, shell, then remove the crankarms with a crank removal tool. (Fig. 4.4g). Next, loosen and completely unscrew the locking nut on the left side of the bottom bracket. (Figs. 4.4h, 4.4i). This will allow the removal of the bearing cup which is threaded into the bottom bracket shell. (Fig. 4.4j). The bearing cup on the chainring side of the bottom bracket—also known as the "fixed cup"—does not have to be removed unless bearing and race wear as evidenced on the opened side indicates replacement of the entire unit. (Figs. 4.4k, 4.4l).

Once the removable bearing cup is out, you'll be able to retrieve the ball bearings (which are usually in a ring cage), the spindle (remember which side came out first as the length of the spindle on the outside of the bearing retainers is different on each side), and the bearings from the fixed cup side. Visually inspect the area noting any metal shavings, pitting off-sided bearings, or signs of brinelling in the cup. You will need to clean the area, repack the bearings in clean grease, then put it all back together the same way it came apart, and then adjust for play. The cranks should spin freely with no "bearing drag," and just the slightest feel of side to side play.

The final bearing adjustment is via the cones and nuts on each axle. The cone holds the bearings in place on either side of the hub. The hub is the area from the spokes inward. (Fig. 4.4m). It contains the axle and bearings, which allow it to spin freely. Any side-to-side movement of the wheel while it is attached to the bicycle indicates loose cones. Remove the wheel from the bicycle to clearly inspect this area. Take hold of the axle and attempt to move it back and forth. Movement indicates looseness. You will notice that just outside the cone is another nut.

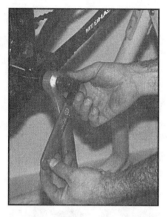

Fig. 4.4g. Using crankarm removal tool

You will need cone wrenches to back the outer nut off the cone nut to make any adjustments. You start by closing (or tightening) down the cone until there is no movement, though it spins smoothly. Take it a quarter turn further, then close down the exterior nut to the cone. (Fig. 4.4o). Holding the exterior nut in place, back off the cone a quarter turn. There should be enough play so you don't feel bearing drag or, resistance, as you spin the wheel while holding the ends of the axle in your fingers. (Fig. 4.4p). There must be a little play because when you install the wheel, tightening the skewer will push inward against the cones and take up some play. Remember, axle cones, headsets and bottom brackets that are over tightened will cause premature bearing wear and failure. Check and re-adjust as many times as it takes to get it right.

Fig. 4.4h. Non-chainring side of an adjustable bottom bracket: A - lockring; B - adjustable bearing cup

There are some repairs you need to understand, but will probably not try to do. Wheel truing, for example, is complex and detail-oriented. It is important to watch your wheels so that as they go out of true, you will know it is time to get them fixed. The best way to develop this skill is to contact your local bike shop and get some pointers. Then take an old wheel and get some hands-on experience. Here are the basics:

If the wheel is just slightly out of true, you can work on it on the bike using the brake blocks as guides to locate the area of the rim that's out of shape as it passes by them. (Fig. 4.4q). However, if the wheel is more than slightly out of true and you don't have access to a truing stand, remove the wheel, take the tire and tube off and then re-install the wheel on the frame. You will find this an easier method than looking over the tire at the brake blocks.

Fig. 4.4i. Removing lockring from adjustable bottom bracket

Fig. 4.4j. Using pinspanner to remove adjustable bearing cup

Fig. 4.4k. Spindle removed revealing bearings on fixed bearing cup side

Fig. 4.4l. Tightening fixed bearing cup

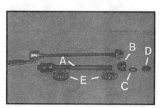

Fig. 4.4m. Hub with one side disassembled: A - axle; B - cone nut; C - washer; D - lock- nut; E - bearings and caps

The rim can be moved back toward center (into true) by tightening and loosening the spoke nipples with the correct size spoke wrench. Tightening the spoke pulls it toward the side of the hub that the spoke is attached to: Loosening it will allow it to move away from that side. (Fig. 4.4r). Once the warped area is located, begin with the spoke in the middle of the section and work, alternately, with the spokes on either side of it for a total of about five spokes. Work in small increments or you may cause more of a problem than you started with. Usually, about one quarter turn on each nipple is sufficient to begin moving the rim to true. Some suggestions:

- A little goes a long way. You should not do more than a half turn of a spoke nipple, without checking the wheel.

- Loosening is as good as tightening, if it corrects the problem. You will not want the spokes to be loose and easy to move, but many times the problem can be solved by loosening slightly.

- Never think adjusting a single spoke will correct the problem. Work the two spokes on either side of the focal point so that the change is mild and spread between five spokes rather than one.

- A wheel that is "out-of-round" or has a flat spot can be saved in many cases, but should be taken to someone who has extensive knowledge of wheel building and proper tools.

Broken spokes should be replaced as soon as possible, but can be dealt with on the road until repairs can be made later. It is helpful to carry a couple of spares in your bag for emergencies (be sure they're the correct length). Spokes usually break at the flange where they are threaded through the hub, so the rest of the spoke can be unthreaded from the nipple and a new one replaced rather easily—unless it's on the gear side of the rear wheel.

If the broken spoke is on the gear side of the rear hub, you will not be able to install the new spoke without removing the gear cluster first—unless you have a special spoke replacement kit that uses a strand of kevlar or wire (tightened by a turnbuckle) to take the place of the spoke. There are several of these new kits on the market now. When on the road or trail, the best thing to do is make sure the tension of the spokes near the broken one is sufficient to hold the rim in place; then "baby it" until you can make repairs. You can either remove the broken spoke or wind it around adjacent spokes to keep it from tangling in the frame as the wheel turns. Avoid curb hops, hook slides, and any maneuver that would put lateral pressure or sudden impact to the rim.

Fig. 4.4n. Rear hub without freewheel showing freehub "A"

Choosing a Bike Shop & Mechanic

If you are not going to be making all the repairs to your bicycle, it is very important to locate an experienced bike shop with high-quality mechanics. There are several factors to consider when choosing a bike shop. The size of the shop can be important. Larger shops will usually have a larger inventory, enabling you to get replacement parts quicker and easier. The quality of the items being sold by the shop is another important factor. If it bills $150 mountain bikes as its top-of-the-line model, the shop probably doesn't offer the high-quality equipment or experience your unit will require. "Pro shops" are on the other extreme. They tend to deal exclusively with $2,000+ mountain bikes or road bikes. A shop which only deals with road bikes may not have staff with the experience necessary to properly meet your needs. These shops sometimes only deal in high-end parts that your agency cannot afford and does not need. Look for a shop with a strong inventory of middle- to high-end quality mountain bikes, certified mechanics, and managers and staff you feel comfortable with.

Fig. 4.4 o. Adjusting the cone and locknuts

Please find Figs. 4.4p and 4.4q on the next page

Negotiate a strong service contract that includes priority turn around. Bike shops in most metropolitan areas keep bikes several days for repairs. Racers and bike commuters who are regular customers and depend on their bikes are often given informal "head of the line" privileges. The shop owner recognizes both their worth as regular customers, and that the bike is more important to

Fig. 4.4r. Every spoke pulls to a different side of the hub; "A" points out a spoke nipple

Fig. 4.4p. Checking for bearing play by holding ends of axle and spinning wheel

Fig. 4.4q. Using the brake pads to perform minor wheel truing with spokewrench

the commuter or racer than to someone who is merely getting a tire fixed for an upcoming weekend ride. It's the sort of triage that goes on in hospital emergency rooms. Since most public safety bike squads have a limited number of bikes, make sure you request the same attention. You may also want to ask about an "open shop" policy for officers who want to learn more about hands-on repair.

Parts and labor should come at some discount. But don't expect a significant break on the price of a bicycle, unless your department is buying a large number of them. The markup on bikes themselves is minimal and the shop has to invest significant labor in each unit, which comes unassembled from the factory. Unlike when buying a car, trying to negotiate bicycle prices down won't get you much more than the clerk's annoyance. It's far more acceptable to negotiate for a better price on accessories, such as helmets and clothing.

POLICE BICYCLE MAINTENANCE — POINTS TO REMEMBER

Be sure you understand the following before cycling:
1. How to conduct a pre-ride safety check.
2. How to perform basic bicycle maintenance and repair.
3. How to troubleshoot.
4. How to effectively handle road repairs.
5. Know when to take the bicycle to a shop.

Realize that from a cost-effective standpoint, your department may prefer to pay an experienced bicycle mechanic to do repairs. In other cases, your department may want to save money by letting officers work on the bicycles during down time. Nevertheless, don't forget these three basic rules:
1. Make sure the right tools are on hand.
2. Always check the basics before going any further.
3. Never try fixing what is not understood.

CHAPTER FIVE:
VEHICULAR CYCLING

R iding a police bicycle may be one of the most enjoyable and productive things you will do during your law enforcement career. It may also be one of the most dangerous. As police officers, we all know of other officers who have been killed or permanently disabled in an on-the-job traffic collision. On a bicycle, you face the possibility of being seriously injured or killed in a vehicular crash. Knowing how to ride your police bicycle in vehicular traffic may make all the difference in terms of your safety and effectiveness. As a police cyclist, you must know how to operate your bicycle predictably, legally, and safely on the roadway when in or near motorized traffic.

> T he basic tenet of vehicular cycling is that cyclists fare best when they act and are treated as drivers of vehicles.

5.1 THE LAW

B efore you can understand bicycling safety, it helps to understand the law. Most states within the U.S. define bicycles as "vehicles," and as vehicle operators, cyclists have a legal right to use the roadway. In the few states which do not define bicycles as vehicles, the laws still read something like, "A person riding a bicycle upon a public roadway has all the rights, and is subject to the same duties and responsibilities, as any other vehicle operator." Whether or not bicycles are defined as vehicles, cyclists in every state have the right to use the roadway. As we progress through this chapter, we shall see that riding on the roadway is not only a cyclist's right, it is the safest place for him or her to operate.

5.2 RULES OF THE ROAD—WHERE, WHAT AND WHY

A re bicycles vehicles? While many people will immediately answer "yes," the answer is often spoken with uncertainty. What is the legal status of bikes in your state or province? Standing before a typical police cyclist class, instructors can "see the wheels turning" while students try to recall from their driver's training or academy days just exactly what was said about bikes. "Something about the rules of the road applying to them, too..." is about as close as most people come. This confusion exists, in part, because there are two different legal definitions of bicycles.

Some states include bicycles in their vehicle or traffic code definition of "vehicles." The code simply exempts bicycles from various laws which do not apply to them, such as requirements for mufflers, bumpers, and turn signal lights.

Some states define bicycles separately, and actually exclude them from their definition of vehicles. When bikes are defined in this manner, cyclists are specifically accorded the same rights and responsibilities as motorists, except for those having no application to bicycles.

Before going any further in studying laws having an influence on bike unit operations, double check the system used to define bicycles in your jurisdiction. A firm grasp of this basic concept is a must before trying to correctly interpret the other laws relative to bicycle operations. Refer to your state and local traffic laws as you go through this section of the book.

What is the legal definition of the following terms when used in your jurisdiction?

- Highway
- Roadway
- Street
- Road
- Sidewalk
- Shoulder
- Bike Lane
- Bike Path
- Bike Route

Bike Lanes, Paths, and Routes

Many people lump together the terms bike path, bike lane, and bike route. However, there are significant differences between them.

Generally, a **bike lane** refers to a section of the roadway designated by painted lines and other markings. A bike lane is a portion of the road, not the sidewalk. One problem with bike lanes is that they seem to suggest to other road users that the cyclist should be riding exclusively in the bike lane. Many jurisdictions require use of the bike lane if one exists, except when making turns or to avoid hazards. (Fig. 5.2a)

A **bike route** is allegedly a route which facilitates bike travel. It may take the cyclist on regular roads, onto sidewalks, bike paths, or bike lanes to accomplish this. It's kind of like an interstate bike highway. You may be on the expressway one minute and the business loop the next. Unfortunately, many bike routes are designed for a meandering family ride with no particular destination. Some motorists think a cyclist using the road is "off the bike route," when in fact they are merely taking a more direct route to their destination.

Bike paths are typically multi-use trails. They are physically set apart from the roadway and can be characterized by their smaller signs and presence of joggers, in-line skaters, equestrians, and dogs, the sworn enemy of cyclists the world over. Though they are away

Fig. 5.2a. Here's a bike lane that puts the cyclist inside of the path of a right turning vehicle

from the road, the presence of so many people traveling at very different speeds can sometimes make bike paths more dangerous than riding on the road.

It is important to understand the difference between these types of cycling paths due to the existence of laws concerning their use. For example, let's assume your state requires cyclists to use **bike lanes** whenever they are present. Perhaps your state also gives cyclists the same duties and responsibilities as motorists.

Suppose a commuting cyclist is traveling along on a strait thoroughfare, averaging 18 mph, and is lawfully positioned along the right side of the road in the **bike lane**. As the road passes a large city park, the **bike lane** disappears, and a **bike path** that meanders through a crowded park takes its place. Not wanting to stray from his direct route to work, or slow for the 15-mph trail speed limit, the cyclist remains on the surface street. A local traffic officer sees the cyclist, stops him, and issues a ticket for not using the "**bike lane**." If the cyclist is astute, he will point out to the officer that a **bike lane** was not present, and therefore, his decision to use the street was a lawful one.

There are states with mandatory side path laws that require cyclists to use bike paths or lanes when present. Unfortunately, bike paths do not serve the needs of everyone riding a bike. To require a cyclist to use a bike path is like requiring a motorist to use a parallel freeway to travel a few blocks when the surface street would be quicker and more convenient. For this reason, laws requiring the use of side paths are under attack from the League of American Bicyclists, and have been repealed in many states.

Local jurisdictions are normally granted authority by state law to regulate cycling on "pedestrian facilities." Whenever state laws recognize bicycles as vehicles, or grants cyclists the same duties and responsibilities of motorists, regulating the riding of bikes on the roadway rests with the state. Many cities and districts overlook this fact when enacting cycling laws, and overstep their authority when they attempt to ban cyclists from certain roadways.

If your job involves enforcing traffic law, you may want to investigate the signs and ordinances relative to bicycles in your area to make sure they are enforceable! Remember, green signs with white letters are informational, not regulatory. Black and white signs are regulatory, but they may have an unlawful message. For example, a sign proclaiming: "Bikes Must Use Sidewalk" may well reflect an ordinance which has no basis in law. In one city with exactly that situation, local cycling groups pressured city hall to change the word "must" to "may" on all such signs. But even with permissive language, these signs are a stick in the spokes of many local cyclists. Why? Since cyclists in that state are allowed on sidewalks unless prohibited by local ordinance, the signs give them permission to do something they are already allowed to do, and encourages something that's actually dangerous. It is sort of like a sign saying, "Stopping at Yellow Light Prohibited." The real harm done by the signs is that they send the message to motorists that cyclists belong on the sidewalk.

Sidewalks

In your area or jurisdiction there are, most likely, many sidewalks. But can you, a uniformed police cyclist ride on them?

This area of the law causes considerable confusion for the public (and police for that matter). It goes back to the definition of bicycles. If your jurisdiction classifies bikes as "vehicles," then the question is, "are vehicles prohibited from driving on sidewalks?" Some state provisions consider bikes operated on sidewalks or crosswalks to be pedestrians, so they are therefore subject to pedestrian rules. Most often, laws that prohibit or restrict the riding of bikes on sidewalks or trails are imposed by local regulation, such as city or county ordinances.

Fig. 5.2b. Police cyclists must often use sidewalks to perform their duties

Some states cleverly skirt the issue. The California Vehicle Code is one good example. Its references to bike travel are fairly vague. Though the California Vehicle Code does not consider bikes "vehicles," it gives cyclists the same responsibilities as motorists, except for "those provisions, which by their very nature, have no application..." In addition, since there is a specific section concerning bicycles which only speaks to the use of the roadway and shoulder, not the entire highway, one could interpret these laws to permit cycling on the sidewalk in any direction.

The Right Solution For The Right Problem

The nature of a public safety officer's work will sometimes, and perhaps often, require riding his or her bicycle across lawns, off designated trails, against traffic, and on sidewalks. (Fig. 5.2b). In other words, in direct violation of most laws regulating the use of bicycles! In addition to being very careful, public safety cyclists should encourage legislative bodies to pass appropriate state and local exemptions to bike laws for uniformed officers.

While the "rules of the road" are substantially similar across the U.S., a wide variety of special rules are adopted locally to regulate bicycles. When examining the ones in your community, remember: If the problem you encounter stems from a state law, you must address the issue at the state level. A municipality or county cannot require motorists to stop for green lights or ignore stop signs. Similarly, a town council resolution proclaiming your bike an "emergency vehicle," normally will not exempt you from the rules of the road. On the other hand, you may very well need local exemptions from local rules, such as park district ordinances prohibiting bike riding on lawns, or a university rule prohibiting bikes inside campus buildings.

Minnesota, the first state to pass Police Cyclist provisions, simply amended the section of the Traffic Code entitled "Operation of Bicycles" § 169.222 to read,

"Peace officers operating bicycles in the course of their duties are exempt form the provisions of this section."

In 1995, California passed the following amendment to its Vehicle Code:

"21200.(a) Every person riding a bicycle upon a highway has all the rights and is subject to all the provisions applicable to the driver of a vehicle by this division, including but not limited to, provisions concerning driving under the influence of alcoholic beverages or drugs,...

(b)(1) Any peace officer, as defined in Chapter 4.5 (commencing with section 830) of Title 3 Part 2 of the Penal Code, operating a bicycle during the course of his or her duties is exempt from the requirements of subdivision (a), except as those requirements relate to driving under the influence of alcoholic beverages or drugs, if the bicycle is being operated under any of the following circumstances:

(A) In response to an emergency call.

(B) While engaged in rescue operations.

(C) In the immediate pursuit of an actual or suspected violator of the law.

(2) This subdivision does not relieve a peace officer from the duty to operate a bicycle with regard for the safety of all persons using the highway.

While the amendment is a step in the right direction, it does not address EMS applications.

Driving Under the Influence

Do the implied consent and driving under the influence statutes apply to bicyclists? If so, how do they differ from motorist requirements? While you may not be planning to work while under the influence, law enforcement bike patrol officers will find themselves coming into contact more often with other cyclists, some of whom will be drunk or under the influence of drugs. Other cops will understandably think bike cops are the experts on the subject, and will look to them for advice when encountering drunk cyclists.

Most states prohibit "drunk driving" on bicycles, although many have reduced fines and penalties for offenses occurring on bikes.

Drunk driving laws often apply to cyclists, while implied consent laws normally apply only to the driving of motor vehicles. Implied consent comes with accepting a driver's license. Since one does not need a driver's license to ride a bicycle, no implied consent has been given. This does not mean that chemical tests can't be offered, or that a refusal can't be used against the defendant in a criminal trial, just that there may be no administrative sanction available against the person's driver's license. The last few years have seen so many drastic changes in public attitude and laws concerning drinking and driving that a careful review of the law as it applies in your situation is a must.

Radios

Many states prohibit the use of headsets, such as a personal stereo by those operating vehicles or riding bikes. Check the codes in your area. Keep this in mind when selecting radio equipment! If your agency uses radio headsets, this may be another area requiring an exemption from state law.

Equipment Requirements

Traffic codes regarding bicycle brakes normally require either the rider to be able to stop within a certain distance when traveling at a specified speed, or to make the rear wheel skid on clean, dry pavement. Brakes on public safety bikes must meet these requirements.

Police cyclist units that work at night, or that may have to ride in reduced visibility conditions (virtually any unit), must have adequate lighting and reflectors. Some states require active red tail lights, and all states permit their use. Fairly universal is the requirement for a red rear reflector visible from 600 feet, side reflectors, such as the ones mounted on spokes, pedal reflectors, and any other reflector required by the Consumer Product Safety Commission (CPSC) for sale with bicycles.

All cyclists should wear properly-fitted helmets while riding. To date, there are no laws in the U.S. requiring adults to wear helmets while cycling. There are, however, a growing number of helmet laws that require juveniles or children to use helmets when riding in bicycle seats. You shouldn't need a law or even a department policy to require you to wear a helmet. You wouldn't hit the street without your firearm, so don't forget your bike helmet!

Audible Signals

Does your state law or local ordinance require an audible signal device on your bicycle? While your city may not, a trail managed by the local park district may require bikes to have a bell or other device when being operated on their paths. Unless authority is granted by the state traffic code, it may be unlawful for a local jurisdiction to require a bike bell on public roadways. Local jurisdictions often forget this fact, and routinely pass laws restricting bicycles with little thought to the status granted them by the state's traffic code. This is equivalent to the laws that prohibit a city or county from changing the meaning of a stop sign.

Fig. 5.2c. Proper hand signals; check and see which "right turn" is legal in your state

Turn Signals

Cyclists normally use the same hand signals as motorists, and use them under the same circumstances. Many states allow cyclists to use an additional signal to indicate a right turn. (Fig. 5.2c). This additional signal is done by extending the right arm horizontally to the right, the opposite of a left turn signal. Remember, perhaps even more important than signaling is looking both ways before turning. Communication must take place between the cyclist and the other users of the highway.

Licensing Requirements

Even if your area does not require bicycle licensing, it is a good idea to do it. It sets a good example, and helps provide a record of the bike. Keep license information on file with other data that can be useful if the bike is subject to manufacturer's recall, is stolen, or needs to be returned to correct a defect or equipment failure.

5.3 ROAD POSITIONING

The basic rules of the road, as listed in your state's traffic code, effect all roadway users, motorized or not. That includes obeying posted signs, traffic signals, and right-of-way rules. Some laws by their very nature do not and cannot effect cyclists. Not even a rookie trooper would cite a bicyclist for illegal bumper height or failure to use a seat belt! But, other laws exist that only affect cyclists.

Every state in the U.S. requires cyclists to ride with the flow of traffic, and in most states, the statutory language requires cyclists to ride "as far right as practicable to the right side of the roadway." Note that the word used is practicable, not practical. Webster's Dictionary defines practicable as "possible to practice or perform." The word implies expectation of successful testing rather than an assurance of proof. For example, one might say "the modern low-slung high-speed automobile was practicable long before improved roads and fuels made it practical."

Note that the law does not require cyclists to ride "as far right as possible." If the law said that, you would see cyclists either riding in the gutter or balanced precariously along the edge of the pavement. As written, the law allows you, the cyclist, to decide the safest place to ride. Interpret the law to mean that cyclists shall ride "as far right as is safe in the appropriate lane."

The decision of where to ride is based upon a number of factors, including:

- Your experience
- Your equipment (road bike or mountain bike)

- Your perception of the dangers
- The condition and width of the roadway
- The presence of bike lanes if use is mandatory
- Allowing 3 to 4 feet of "wobble space"
- The likelihood of a pedal striking the curb
- Movements you anticipate making within the lane (e.g. preparing for a vehicular style left turn)

How Far Right Is Far Enough?

Just how far to the right should cyclists ride? Bicycles are single-track vehicles that require balance to remain upright. Cyclists balance by subtly moving the front wheel back and forth. Imagine balancing a baseball bat upright in the palm of your hand. You make delicate movements back and forth to maintain balance. Cyclists do the same thing with their front wheel. The resulting wobble is more noticeable at slow speeds than at higher speeds. Generally, cyclists should allow a 3-foot wide *wobble* lane for them to travel safely. (Fig. 5.3a). If riding on a road with a curb and gutter, the joint—where the asphalt and concrete gutter apron meet—would be on the right side of that lane. The wobble lane would not be right next to the curb. Likewise, if riding on a paved shoulder that tends to accumulate sand and other debris, your wobble lane would be to the left side of the debris. Some experienced cyclists choose to ride just to the left of the fog line, regardless of the width of the shoulder. Realize that some motorists may get upset when cyclists are riding in their lane when there is an 8-foot wide paved shoulder to ride on. Normally riding just to the right of the fog line is sufficient to ride on good pavement while staying away from debris.

Fig. 5.3a. Your "wobble" lane should allow safe clearance of storm grates and other obstacles

Exceptions to Riding On the Far Right

Cyclists do not have to constantly ride on the far-right side of the road. Statutes allow you to leave the right side under the following circumstances:

- When making a turning movement
- When passing a slower moving vehicle or bicycle

- To avoid a hazard
- When the width of the street makes it unsafe (this is especially true in situations where riding close to the roadway edge would encourage a driver to pass despite insufficient room to do so).

A defensive cyclist will keep their eyes moving constantly, searching 3 to 4 seconds ahead of them. If a hazard such as a rock or pot hole is spotted, the cyclist would have time to scan behind them and be sure it is safe to move to the left into the traffic lane. If spotted too late or there is a vehicle approaching, the cyclist must use a *rock dodge* maneuver to avoid the hazard. In this maneuver, a cyclist steers his front wheel far around the hazard and then back into his original riding line, forcing the back wheel to also swerve around the object. When approaching a parked vehicle, or line of parked vehicles, try to determine if they are occupied. If the vehicle is occupied, there is a strong possibility that a car door could open or the vehicle may pull out in front of you. When approaching a parked car search to the rear and determine if it is safe to move to the left into the traffic lane. If it isn't safe, stop. If it is clear, move to the left and maintain a line that is just to the left of any car door that might open in front of you. If there are gaps in the parked cars, hold your line until you have passed all of the parked cars. Holding your line is far more predictable to drivers who are overtaking you.

Remember, when moving away from the roadway edge, always look, signal, and continue to look and signal as often as needed to ensure safety and communication between you and other users of the road.

5.4 RIDING DEFENSIVELY AND ASSERTIVELY

Inexperienced, untrained cyclists are often timid riding in or near traffic. Experienced, trained cyclists understand they have a right to use the roadway as a part of traffic. Skilled cyclists ride both defensively and assertively. These two styles are not counterproductive. A defensive cyclist is always alert and anticipates the mistakes of other drivers around them. They are prepared to evade or stop for obstacles or vehicles that threaten them. An assertive cyclist understands they are part of traffic and operate within the rules. An assertive cyclist will take the entire traffic lane if necessary, they will signal and request right of way from motorists, and generally operate as they would in their car.

Fig. 5.4a. Ride at least a car door length away from those parked cars

As a police cyclist you must be both defensive and assertive. When cycling in a police uniform you will enjoy a respect from motorists most cyclists only dream of. As officer Allan Howard of the Dayton, Ohio Police Department says, "Drivers would sooner cross the yellow line and hit a utility pole than breeze a cop on a bike." That allows you to be especially assertive when necessary to get to a hot call, or catch up to a suspect vehicle. Don't forget that not every motorist sees cyclists—police uniform or not—and you must still remain defensively vigilant.

The Dangers of Wrong-Way Riding

Riding against traffic is not only wrong, it's extremely dangerous for a number of reasons. An unexpected roadway position, coupled with a bike's speed, removes you from the scanning pattern of the majority of motorists. (Fig. 5.4a). Based on habit and experience, many motorists are focused on on-coming traffic, positioning wrong-way cyclists in a motorist "blind spot." By riding against traffic, you increase your chances of getting into an accident. Wrong-way riders are involved in nearly one-third of all bicycle/motor vehicle crashes. Wrong-way riders also pose a threat to cyclists who are riding legally. When appearing from behind parked cars or other cyclists, wrong-way riders can be involved in a head-on crash with closing speeds up to 40 mph. This can easily be a fatal crash for either cyclist. Fear of vehicles approaching you from behind does not justify riding against traffic. In his book *Effective Cycling*, John Forester points out some interesting facts about this fear:

"New cyclists fear that they will be hit from behind by fast motorists, almost to the exclusion of any other fear of motor traffic. This fear is created by parents, teachers, police officers, motor-vehicle driver education, and other social forces. However, this fear is entirely unwarranted, because about 90 percent of car-bike collisions are caused by conditions or actions in front of the cyclist, where they can be seen and therefore avoided by proper avoidance actions. Of the 10 percent of accidents that are caused by conditions behind the cyclist, 6 percent are caused by the cyclist swerving in front of the car and only 4 percent by the overtaking motorist. Of this 4 percent, half are caused by motorists who do not see the cyclist (generally in the dark) and often by motorists who have been drinking; some by motorists who misjudge the width of their vehicles, and very few by motorists who are out of control."

Riding on the wrong side of the street also prevents cyclists from seeing the signs and traffic control devices meant for traffic traveling in their direction. Riding in a predictable, lawful manner increases personal safety by maximizing the opportunity for other drivers to see and respond to you as a vehicle.

The Speed Positioning Principle

When cycling on a roadway, it is important that you adhere to the speed positioning principle. This principle dictates that the slowest moving vehicles operate in the far-right lane and the fastest vehicles operate in the far left. At times you will be the slowest vehicle on the road, and must ride on the right side. Other times, like when descending a hill or riding in crowded urban traffic, you will be as fast as the other traffic. In that case take the entire lane. Just remember, if you are riding in the far-left lane on a two-lane road, the fastest vehicles will be passing in the oncoming lane.

One exception to these lane positioning rules would occur on a very narrow roadway that would not allow a cyclist and a motor vehicle to pass safely side by side within the same lane. While an inexperienced cyclist would move as far right as possible in an attempt to make room for the motorist to pass, a skilled cyclist would move to the left—taking the entire lane—to force the motorist to pass him legally, using the oncoming lane. By trying to make room for the motorist to pass, the cyclist may ride down in the debris-filled gutter, trap a tire in the joint separating the asphalt and gutter apron, strike their pedal on top of the curb or set up any one of several fall provoking events. Cyclists have the right to the lane if they need it—so take it if necessary.

Fig. 5.4b. Be careful! The dangers of passing on the right here are many.

Fig. 5.4c. This may be the safer option.

Passing

Whether passing a motor vehicle or another cyclist, it is always safest to pass on the left. Passing a slower vehicle on the right could result in your being trapped if the vehicle suddenly turns right or pulls to the shoulder. Giving an audible or verbal warning, such as "passing on your left," to alert the other driver may be advisable before you pass them.

Cyclists may find themselves in heavy traffic that backs up from controlled intersections. If there is room on the right side of the line for you to safely pass you may do so. (Fig. 5.4b). Motorists may get very agitated if they are passed by the cyclist at the intersection, only to pass the cyclist mid-block and get passed again at the next intersection. Cyclists who are able to ride at or near the same speed as other traffic would be better off taking the lane and getting in line with the other traffic. (Fig. 5.4c). Experienced cyclists try to pass the same cars at an intersection only once.

One-Third of the Lane Rule

Another basic rule in cycling is the *one-third of the lane rule*. When approaching an intersection cyclists

Fig. 5.4d.

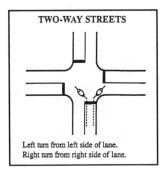

Fig. 5.4e.

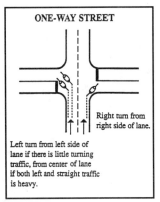

Fig. 5.4f.

should occupy the one-third portion of the lane that is nearest their destination. For example, if you are approaching an intersection where you will make a right turn, you should be in the right one-third of the lane. If you are stopping at a controlled intersection and plan to go straight, you should stop in the middle one-third of the lane. (Fig. 5.4d). That will allow room for right turn on red drivers to pass easily. After starting out from the sign or signal move to the portion of the road that is most appropriate to your speed, according to the speed positioning principle. (Fig. 5.4e). A cyclist who is making a left turn at the intersection should stay on the left side of the lane, close to the center line. (The middle of a lane where cars and trucks stop at intersections may get slippery due to oil drippings. This is especially true when it is raining. Cyclists should choose to stay to the left of the center, even when going straight, because of this problem.) That will signal the cyclist's intent to motorists and will allow room for motorists, who are going straight, to pass on the right of the cyclist without causing any delays. (Fig. 5.4f).

Cyclists and motorists are safer and more predictable when they make turns from the lane nearest their destination. Traffic law requires vehicles to change course from the correct lane. A cyclist, or any other vehicle, making a sudden left turn at an intersection from the right side of the road is acting very unpredictably. Left turning vehicles should move into the left lane, or the left turn lane if provided, before changing their course. Bicycles are no exception, as mentioned earlier. Bicycles may legally leave the right side of the road to make a left turn. Skilled cyclists preparing for a left turn will search to the rear before moving left. They set up the turn well in advance, depending on the volume and speed of adjacent traffic and the number of traffic lanes. When there is a gap in traffic, they will signal and move toward the center line. Once near the center line they can signal their turn and wait for a gap in oncoming traffic, if necessary. Overtaking cars can pass on the cyclist's right. In this position, the cyclist is visible, predictable and communicating to other traffic his intention to turn left. In this case, the cyclist is both acting and being treated as the driver of a vehicle.

Channelized Intersections

If the intersection is channelized with turning lanes, the skilled, vehicular-style cyclist will use them. Many inexperienced cyclists feel uncomfortable leaving the right-side edge, regardless of what type of lane it is. (Fig. 5.4g). If there is a right-turn-only lane, they will still ride on the right side and go straight at the intersection. If a motorist did that in front of us, they would risk getting a ticket. This is a frequent violation for cyclists and it creates a very unpredictable situation at intersections. How many officers think about enforcing it when the violator is on a bike? The proper way to proceed straight when a right-turn-only lane is present is to ride in the right one-third of the straight through lane. Often this is just to the left of the right-turn-only lane. If there are two right-turn-only lanes, the right turning cyclist should ride in the lane closest to the right-turn lane.

When making a left turn with a left turn only lane, you must safely cross the through lanes and get into the right one-third of the left turn only lane. (Fig. 5.4h). Then, after completing the turn, you will already be positioned in the right one third of the new roadway. If there are two or more left turn lanes, you must ride in the right-most turn lane.

Some intersections have multiple destination lanes. (Fig. 5.4i). Cyclists approaching these lanes need to remember the basic vehicular cycling rule requiring them to ride in the right-most lane that goes to their destination, while following the one-third of the lane rule. If a cyclist is using a multiple destination lane, they must position their bike in the appropriate one-third of the lane, according to their destination.

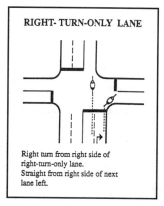

RIGHT- TURN-ONLY LANE

Right turn from right side of right-turn-only lane.
Straight from right side of next lane left.

Fig. 5.4g.

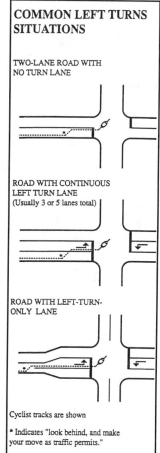

COMMON LEFT TURNS SITUATIONS

TWO-LANE ROAD WITH NO TURN LANE

ROAD WITH CONTINUOUS LEFT TURN LANE
(Usually 3 or 5 lanes total)

ROAD WITH LEFT-TURN-ONLY LANE

Cyclist tracks are shown

* Indicates "look behind, and make your move as traffic permits."

Fig. 5.4h.

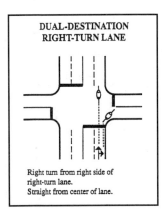

DUAL-DESTINATION
RIGHT-TURN LANE

Right turn from right side of
right-turn lane.
Straight from center of lane.

Fig. 5.4i.

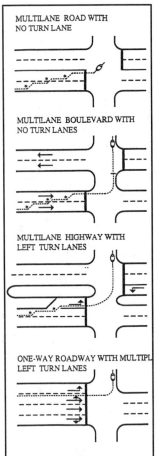

MULTILANE ROAD WITH
NO TURN LANE

MULTILANE BOULEVARD WITH
NO TURN LANES

MULTILANE HIGHWAY WITH
LEFT TURN LANES

ONE-WAY ROADWAY WITH MULTIPL
LEFT TURN LANES

Fig. 5.4j.

Merging and Lane Changing

Experienced cyclists are constantly aware of the traffic around them. In addition to keeping their eyes constantly searching ahead, they also do rear scans, sometimes called *shoulder checks*, to monitor the traffic behind them. (Fig. 5.4j). Most bicycle/motor vehicle crashes involve events happening in front of the bicyclist. But a cyclist who pulls into a lane of traffic, without first checking to see if it is clear, is greatly increasing their chance of being struck by an overtaking vehicle. This is statistically one of the most deadly crash types. It doesn't matter if you are on duty and covered by worker's compensation, it is imperative that you understand how to safely merge and change lanes.

We will start with a simple lane change on a single lane with low volume traffic. Anticipate the need for the lane change ahead of time to avoid being rushed. Each lane crossed will require two shoulder checks and two moves to the left. You start by checking over your shoulder for traffic. If traffic is far enough back, and not overtaking rapidly, signal your move with an extended left arm. If traffic is close by, but moving slowly, an extended arm may be a way of requesting permission to move in front of them. The faster motorist has the right-of-way to that lane. They may or may not allow you to pull in front of them. After determining it is safe to move into traffic, pull into the center of the lane. Perform another shoulder check before making the second move to the left side of the lane.

On multiple lanes of traffic the technique is the same. Perform two shoulder checks and two steering movements for each lane crossed. Normally, you should cross one lane of traffic at a time. If there is high-speed traffic or very heavy traffic with infrequent breaks, it may be necessary to cross more than one lane of traffic at a time. Doing so requires great caution and care.

If you are merging from the left side of the road, trying to get to the right side of the roadway, it will obviously require you to shoulder check over your right shoulder. Therefore, you must be able to control your bike while looking over either shoulder.

Occasionally, the lane or shoulder on which you are riding will come to an end or merge with another lane. (Fig. 5.4k). The technique required in this instance is the same: scan to the rear and make the move. If the movement is less than one-lane width, one look and one move may be all that is necessary.

5.5 COMMON CYCLING HAZARDS

Cyclists generally have to deal with three categories of hazards: surface, visual and moving hazards. A skilled and defensive cyclist will look for and antici-pate these hazards and will deal with them accordingly.

Surface Hazards

A *surface hazard* is an obstacle on the riding sur-face that can cause the cyclist to lose control or fall. Surface hazards can be found on roadways, sidewalks, trails, and off-road areas. Common surface hazards include potholes, railroad tracks, sewer grates, broken glass, sand and gravel, expansion joints, pavement cracks, the joint where the concrete gutter apron meets the asphalt roadway, and miscellaneous objects, such as dead animals, car parts, and tree branches.

A seldom recognized hazard is the curb itself. If the cyclist rides too close to the curb, the inside pedal may actually come down on top of it. If this happens, the bike will likely be launched upward and to the left as the pedal pushes down against the curb. This can result in instant disaster if you fall in front of oncoming traffic. A cyclist who avoids riding in the gutter can eas-ily avoid striking the curb and other hazards commonly found there. Cyclists who feel they need to ride as far to the right as possible, or are attempting to make room for traffic to pass on a narrow roadway may find themselves

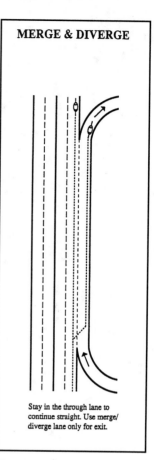

MERGE & DIVERGE

Stay in the through lane to continue straight. Use merge/diverge lane only for exit.

Fig. 5.4k.

Fig. 5.5a.

riding in the gutter. Realize there are many hazards found there and avoid the gutter if at all possible!

Sand, gravel, wet leaves, metal plates, manhole covers, painted areas on the roadway and similar items can cause a bicycle to lose traction and fall. This is especially true if the cyclist is attempting to turn, brake, or accelerate. If these areas are spotted ahead of time, it may be possible to simply ride around them. If they are unavoidable, try to go straight through them, while remaining as upright as possible. If feasible, coast through the area. If the area is too large to coast through, pedal cautiously. You can prevent the rear wheel from skidding out of control by using a gear that can be pedaled softly.

Roads often collect sand and other slippery surface hazards at intersections. If you turn sharply on one of these sandy corners, it's likely your wheels will go out from underneath you. Defensive riders look for these areas as they approach. It may be possible to ride through the area, and make the turn on the far side of it. Other times you may be able to initiate the turn before reaching the hazard, enabling you to ride straight and upright in the slippery area. If you need to slow down, you should brake before the turn. Never apply the brakes during a turn. This is true whether the surface is slippery or not. The small area of the tire in contact with the ground is not large enough to provide the traction necessary to both slow the bike and allow it to turn. This is especially true if a surface hazard is present!

Sewer grates may present a hazard to cyclists if the grates parallel the direction the bike is heading and are wide enough to "swallow" the tire. (Fig. 5.5a). Fortunately this is less of a problem for the wide tires found on mountain bikes than it is for narrower road and touring tires. If your wheel does get trapped, you will be vaulted over your handlebars and onto the ground in milliseconds, a fall known in cycling circles as an *endo* (end over end). Only a helmet and lots of luck will prevent injury if an endo occurs. These crashes can be prevented by watching for and avoiding these grates.

A similar type of crash occurs when your wheel becomes trapped in a parallel crack, or butts against the side of an object such as a curb or railroad track. The front wheel is crucial to your ability to remain upright, because you balance by steering in the opposite direction that the bike is falling. This is a constant, subtle process. Any object which causes your wheel to divert in a direction opposite your point of balance can cause a *diversion fall*. As with all surface hazard-related crashes, they are more easily prevented through avoidance than any other way. Stay away from parallel cracks in riding surfaces. Cross over cracks, railroad tracks and ridges as close to a 90-degree angle as possible. (Fig. 5.5b). Stop pedaling with your pedals in a horizontal position. If riding over a bump, rise off the saddle and use your legs and arms to absorb the shock.

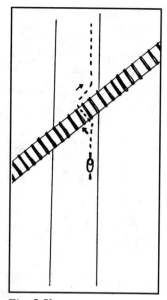

Fig. 5.5b.

Cyclists may experience a diversion fall if trying to escape a deep crack that has their wheel trapped, or when trying to get back on to the paved surface which is at a higher grade than the one they are riding on. This can be a scary experience. If you ride off the paved surface or get a wheel trapped and cannot stop, it is best to make the move to escape quickly and sharply. If you try to slowly climb up onto the pavement or out of the crack your likelihood of "diverting" increases. In the event you ride off the pavement, try to move away from the pavement edge a foot or two before attempting any ascending move. Then turn at a sharp angle (about 45 degrees) back onto the pavement. A cyclist caught in a wide crack must make the move out of the crack just as sharply and quickly. These moves must be done with the same kind of attention used when ascending curbs or other obstacles. Some cyclists may be able to jump or *wheelie hop* out of the crack. Police bikes are usually too heavy to allow the rider to perform a *bunny hop*. Many times it may be safer to simply stop as

Fig. 5.5c. "Rock dodging" an obstacle

Fig. 5.5d. Back wheel will track behind path of front wheel

quickly and safely as possible to avoid a fall from one of these potential *diverters*.

Many surface hazards, like debris in the road, rocks, or small potholes can be avoided by simply steering around them. That is why it's necessary for you to keep sufficient watch ahead. If you fail to notice them until the last instant, a *rock dodging* technique can be employed to move the bike around them. (Figs. 5.5c, 5.5d). That will keep you from swerving out in front of any overtaking traffic, a common cause of potentially fatal overtaking crashes.

Visual Hazards

Visual hazards prevent cyclists and motorists from seeing one another. They also effect the cyclist's ability to see the riding surface and other hazards found in their riding environment. Environmental visual hazards include darkness, fog, rain, and glare. Visual screens are objects that block a person's view. Common visual screens include parked cars, hedges, buildings, groups of pedestrians, and hills. (Fig. 5.5e).

Cycling in low-light conditions can be extremely dangerous. A large percentage of fatal bicycle crashes occur during darkness. Cyclists, including police cyclists, must strive to be as conspicuous as possible when riding in traffic after dark. There will certainly be times when you may want to be inconspicuous for tactical reasons, but cycling in traffic is preferably not one of them. Motorists must see bicyclists in order to avoid crashing into them.

Besides using the required equipment mentioned earlier in this chapter, police cyclists find it useful to use other *conspicuity* devices. This may include LED flashers and reflective material on uniforms or equipment. Research has shown that objects which are unusually bright and are moving or flashing attract the attention of drivers more quickly. (Figs. 5.5f, 5.5g). Pedal reflectors, which show movement, are a very effective nighttime conspicuity device. Be sure that your police bike is equipped with pedal reflectors if it is used at night. Original equipment reflectors break off frequently with the sort of heavy use that police riders give them. It is advisable to replace the reflector with a strip of white or yellow reflective tape. Tape is very durable and provides an inexpensive solution. Cyclists who realize a motorist is overtaking them should make sure they are pedaling, even if it is slowly, so the pedal reflectors will provide movement and increased effectiveness.

Fig. 5.5e. Pedestrians, parked vehicles, vehicles in traffic, and buildings at the intersection are among the visual hazards here

Battery-powered active lights are usually brighter and more effective than reflectors. By combining active taillights with strategically placed reflective material, a cyclist can create a *signature*, or distinct outline of moving pedals and a human shape, that enables the motorist to recognize as quickly as possible that there is a bicyclist ahead. This is essential for safety when riding at night. Because of the increased danger of bicycling in traffic at night, cyclists can never have too many conspicuity devices mounted on the back of the bike or themselves.

Some officers are more comfortable avoiding roadways at certain times of night, regardless of their equipment. They instead use sidewalks, alleys, or parking lots to get where they need to go. Police cyclists usually know if they work in one of these types of areas and what is best for their safety and survival. Officer survival always starts with an awareness of one's environment and the use of common sense as a guide.

Fog, rain, and glare are conditions that, like darkness, substantially reduce visibility. Cyclists riding in fog or rain in the daylight may choose to use their bicycle's headlight to enhance their visibility to drivers ahead of them. Traffic vests or florescent colored uniform parts will also help make police cyclists more visible.

Fig. 5.5f. Using conspicuity devices to create that signature image

Officers riding in the fog or rain at night are up against a number of factors which make cycling on the roadway very dangerous. Rain, fog, blurry wipers and glare from oncoming headlights will reduce a driver's ability to see a cyclist. The cyclist might just as well be

Fig. 5.5g. Headlights should be a minimum of 10 watts

Fig. 5.5h. Watch the front tires for an indication of a turn

invisible! Police cyclists forced to ride in these conditions would be wise to avoid using the roadway, if possible, and use other available routes of travel. If there are no sidewalks or off-road options, choose a route that has fewer cars and slower travel speeds, like a lightly traveled residential street.

Glare is a common condition that is especially dangerous to cyclists at those times when the sun is low on the horizon. Motorists can be easily blinded by the sun and may be able to see only a portion of a driving lane as they are searching for traffic. The driver may see just enough to feel assured that no other motorist is approaching, but it is very easy for a cyclist to get lost in the glare. Certain conditions can compound these problems. Dirty, hazy, or bug-smeared windshields intensify the effects of glare, regardless of whether it is glare from the sun or oncoming headlights.

Cyclists need to be aware of the effects of glare and when it may be a factor. Glare is a frequent cause of car/bike crashes that occur when a motorist makes a left turn in front of a straight-through cyclist, or when an overtaking motorist turns right in front of a cyclist they just passed. Being aware of the position of the sun and your direction of travel in relation to it can help you avoid these mishaps. If the sun is on the horizon behind you, it is possible that an oncoming motorist may not see you. Pay attention to oncoming drivers who appear to be slowing. Not all motorists use their turn signals as required, so watching for turning front tires is often a good tip-off the car is making a left turn. Skilled cyclists anticipate motorists turning in front of them and ride defensively, prepared to use emergency handling techniques if necessary.

Motorists driving into the sun may also have a hard time seeing cyclists traveling in the same direction. You need to be cognizant of this hazard and stay a bit further to the right. Use extra caution at intersections and those places where motorists are likely to make turning or merging movements. Anytime a car overtakes you and appears to slow down, watch its front tires. (Fig. 5.5h). This is the best warning that the motorist is turning right in front of the bicycle. The best defense may either be an emergency (panic) brake to stop or an instant turn to the right to stay on the inside of the motorist.

Glare also increases the probability of motorists pulling away from stop signs, driveways or alleys in front of cyclists they are unable to see. Be mindful of the possibility and ride defensively.

Hills present a unique hazard. While riding up long or steep hills, a cyclist may become fatigued and distracted. After cresting the hill, most cyclists are eager to enjoy the effortless speed the hill provides and often take the traffic lane to do so. As you approach the speed of other traffic, taking the lane is normally suggested. In this case, however, the hill is a visual screen and creates an exception to the *take the lane* rule. Motorists crest the hill at much higher speeds than cyclists and may be startled to suddenly see a slower moving cyclist in the middle of the driving lane. This is especially hazardous on high-speed roadways. Skilled cyclists stay a bit further to the right side of the lane until they are far enough away from the hill's crest to give overtaking motorists time to see them and react appropriately.

Other types of visual hazards you need to be aware of are physical objects which obstruct your view. Commonly called *visual screens*, these hazards include shrubbery, parked vehicles, buildings, pedestrians, hills and similar objects. As with other visual hazards, recognition of the hazard is the most important part of dealing with it. Once a screen is noted, you can make adjustments in your riding or searching technique to either overcome the obstacle or prepare for possible consequences, like cars pulling out unexpectedly.

Moving Hazards

Moving hazards, as the name implies, are anything that moves and which may collide with cyclists or cause them to fall. Common moving hazards include cars,

Fig. 5.5i. Passing a presumably unoccupied car at least a car door length away

other bicycles, pedestrians, in-line skaters, and animals (particularly dogs.)

Parked cars can be considered a moving hazard, even though they are stationary. A car door that opens suddenly or a car that pulls out from a parking spot are both considered moving hazards. When approaching parked cars the police cyclist needs to look into the interior for any passengers or other indicators that the car is occupied. Indicators include brake light flashes, visible exhaust, or a door that is ajar. Defensive cyclists usually treat all parked cars as occupied. (Fig. 5.5i). This means that they scan to the rear and move out into the traffic lane at least one door's width away from the vehicle. This helps a cyclist avoid a crash or a sudden and unpredictable swerve around the door, should it open suddenly. Riding a door's width away from the vehicle doesn't relieve the cyclist of the obligation of searching for occupants, however. Occupants and other pedestrians can still appear suddenly.

If there are a number of cars parked along the street, with wide gaps between them, inexperienced cyclists— who like to stay as far right as they can—will weave around them. (Fig. 5.5j). Skilled cyclists will maintain the line they used when passing the previous vehicles and stay in that line until they have passed all of them. This way, they are not hidden from view between two cars.

A moving hazard can include other bicyclists—particularly the people you ride with everyday. The most common and serious type of crash occurs when the cyclists allow their wheels to overlap while riding single file. If the front rider should make a sudden lateral move to avoid an object on the roadway, for example, and bump the overlapped front wheel of the rear rider, the result can be catastrophic. A type of *diversion* crash usually occurs where the balance of the rear cyclist is suddenly and unexpectedly diverted. Only extreme luck and skill can prevent a fall. Awareness and prevention are the best remedy.

As such, don't draft another cyclist unless both of you are skilled cyclists. To draft correctly, you must be no more than 4 feet from the front rider's back wheel. At higher speeds riding that close doesn't allow cyclists much time for error. The front cyclist must ride at a steady speed and avoid unexpected coasting, slowing or swerves. They must also communicate with their partner behind them, letting them know they are slowing down or avoiding a hazard. This can be done verbally or with hand signals. Should the rear rider find himself getting too close or overlapping wheels, he must take action immediately to correct the problem. Sitting up straighter while coasting—so the wind catches your body —may slow you sufficiently. It may be necessary to gently apply your brakes to slow down. If you are riding as part of a paceline and have other cyclists riding behind you, it is very important that you brake very gently and communicate your action to those behind you. Anyone who has ever watched a bicycle race has probably witnessed how easily chain reaction crashes can occur when cyclists are riding closely to one another.

Crashes and conflicts between cyclists can occur when cyclists are making the transition from double to single file or back. There are several ways that transitions can be safely performed. Communication between riders is always a prerequisite whichever the method used. Everyone must know what they are to do and what the other riders will be doing. Laws of physics can create bad situations for cyclists who try to occupy the same space at the same time!

The most common and dangerous moving hazard police cyclists will encounter are motor vehicles. Almost all of the conflicts between motorists and bicycles occur at intersections and driveways, where the motorists are turning or pulling out into traffic. Skilled cyclists are often able to minimize these conflicts by riding assertively, yet defensively. Once you have spotted a vehicle that is turning, or may pull out in front of you, put your hands near the brake levers. Though prepared

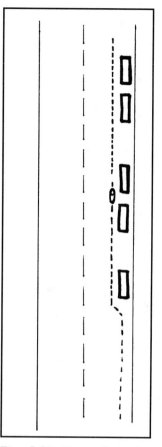

Fig. 5.5j. The cyclist maintains a line until both parked cars and gaps are passed

to stop quickly, if necessary, you should also be assertive as to your right to the road. You can do this by continuing to pedal while holding your line. The term *hold your line* simply means stay in the straight line you are in, without moving to the right or left. Should you quit pedaling the motorist may get the impression you are turning or slowing to allow them to pull out. By continuing to pedal, you are communicating your intent to proceed straight through the intersection.

The same message can be communicated to oncoming drivers who wish to turn left in front of you. If you stop pedaling, the motorist may think you are turning right or yielding to them so that they can turn. Continue pedaling assertively, but keep your hands near the brake levers in case they are needed.

Vehicles turning in front of a cyclist create a very common bicycle/motor vehicle crash scenario. Cyclists can do several things to reduce the chances of this type of crash:

First, enhance conspicuity. Wear clothing or accessories that are bright or contrasting and cause you to stand out. Police cyclists may be somewhat limited in their uniform options. Some administrators insist bike patrol officers wear the same uniform every other police officer wears, with the exception of shorts and a bicycle helmet. If the uniform is a solid dark color or solid tan or brown the police cyclist may tend to fade into the background and be unseen by motorists. Consider using a helmet, epaulets, or other uniform accessories with a contrasting—even bright—color to help you stand out in traffic. Wearing a shirt and shorts of different colors offers a contrast that will stand out and increase conspicuity.

Second, always ride with traffic. Riding against traffic increases your chance of experiencing virtually every type of car/bike crash. There may be times when you have to ride against traffic for tactical or other duty-related reasons. Recognize the danger, particularly at intersections and driveways, and be careful.

Lastly, you need to be vigilant for this type of crash. Watch for oncoming cars that appear to be slowing, whether or not they are signaling for a turn. As with cars overtaking you and slowing, watch the front tires to see if they begin to turn. If it is safe to do so, visually or audibly signal to the driver to make sure you are seen. A wave of a hand or shriek of a whistle, followed by the familiar traffic cop's stop signal may be all that is necessary to alert the driver of your presence. The defensive cyclist will still keep hands near the brake levers and keep pedaling. Should the motorist turn anyway, you may choose to panic brake or instant turn with the motorist. If the oncoming car turns left in front of the bike, the cyclist should instantly turn right, going the same direction as the vehicle. If an overtaking vehicle turns right in front of the bike, the cyclist should instantly turn right to stay on the inside of the vehicle. If this happens, the final thing to do is blow your whistle and signal the motorist to stop. Being able to write them a citation for failing to yield the right-of-way is one of the best parts of being a police cyclist. It's the part of your job avid cyclists most envy!

Hazard Recognition & Common Crashes— Points to Remember

Only 15 percent of all bike crashes resulting in death or injury are a result of a collision with a motor vehicle. Most injuries are a result of falls or collision with pedestrians, dogs, or other cyclists. Common types include:

1. Bike overturn
2. Bike off-road
3. Bike/Fixed object
4. Bike/Bike
5. Bike/Pedestrian
6. Bike/Dog

Police are called to a very small percentage of the bicycle crashes involving injuries.

1. In most states, if they don't involve a motor vehicle, they do not generate an accident report or statistic.

2. It is estimated that only 1 of every 10 bicycle crashes involving injuries is reported.

When car/bike crashes do occur, nearly half of those that are fatal occur at night or in low light conditions. And 75 to 80 percent of the cyclists killed or permanently disabled involve head or neck injuries.

In order to prevent falls, collisions, related injuries or death, it is important for police cyclists to recognize the common hazards and crash types affecting cyclists.

Hazard Recognition

Hazards affecting cyclists are generally broken into three categories: surface, visual and moving.

Common surface hazards include:

1. Holes/cracks/road edge deterioration or drop off
2. Curb/gutter joints or grade differences
3. Curb tops
4. Loose sand/debris/glass
5. Skewed railroad or trolley tracks
6. Expansion joints
7. Drainage grates
8. Standing water/puddles
9. Other

Common visual hazards include:

1. Sun/glare
2. Parked or moving vehicles
3. Fences/landscaping vegetation
4. Buildings
5. Pedestrians
6. Weather/environmental conditions (fog, smoke, wind)
7. Darkness

Common moving hazards include:

1. Motor vehicles
2. Other cyclists/wrong-way cyclists
3. Open car doors

4. "Parked" cars pulling out
5. Pedestrians
6. Dogs, animals

Common Car/Bike Crashes

The most common car/bike crashes involving adult cyclists are:

1. **Motorist unexpected turn.** (The most common adult car/bike crashes.)
- Motorist left turn—oncoming.
- Motorist right turn—parallel paths.
- Motorist left turn—wrong-way cyclist or riding to the left of the motorist.

2. **Motorist overtaking—motorist strikes cyclist from behind.** (The most frequent fatal crash.)
- Bicycle not seen—improper lights/reflectors.
- Motorist out of control—DUI.
- Motorist taking counteractive measures.
- Motorist misjudged space—improper passing.
- Cyclist's path blocked—evading an object and entering the motorist's path.

3. **Motorist stop and go.**
- Motorist disobeys traffic control device at an intersection.
- Motorist fails to yield right-of-way when exiting an alley or driveway.

CONCLUSION

"Bicyclists fare best when they act and are treated as drivers of vehicles."
- John Forester

In order to abide by this basic tenent for safe, effective, cycling, the cyclist must understand all aspects of road positioning, rules of the road, common cycling hazards, and the laws pertaining to both cyclists and motorists in their riding area.

CHAPTER SIX:
TECHNICAL CYCLING

6.1 BIKE FIT

The fit of a bicycle is so crucial that it is better to ride a department store bicycle that fits, than one that costs $1,200 and doesn't fit. Half of all bicycle accidents involve no one but the rider and his or her bicycle. A major contributing factor in a good portion of those accidents is improper bicycle fit. Proper fit starts with buying the right size frame and making adjustments from there. If you don't have the right size frame, there is nothing you can do to make the bike work well. You can make it work, but not well.

Bicycle size is measured by its frame, not its wheels, as many assume. Bicycle frames are measured from the center of the bottom bracket to the top or center of the top tube according to the country of origin. A bicycle that measures 18 inches is an "18," no matter how large or small the wheels are. A proper frame fit on a mountain bike will allow the rider, while straddling the bike, to lift the bike until the top tube touches the body and have both wheels off the ground by at least three to four inches. (Fig. 6.1a). You can get away with less clearance than that, but you'd better stick to smooth roads if you do.

The reason for this is that uneven pavement or terrain automatically subtracts an inch or two from your inseam when you put your foot down. You don't have to be good at math to understand why riding a bike that's too big is a bad idea... Ouch! It's important to remember that if purchasing/sizing a bike with a sloping top

Fig. 6.1a. Proper police mountain bike frame clearance

tube, you'll no doubt have plenty of step-over clearance, just be sure that the rest of the bike "fits" you, meaning the distance from the seat tube to the head tube and the length of the seat tube are correct for your physical dimensions. You want to avoid being too stretched out or cramped up in your riding position. If you're not sure, have a knowledgeable salesperson assist you in selecting the correct fame size for that particular model.

It's important to know how to adjust a bicycle to fit properly. It is possible to make these adjustments while someone holds you up on the bicycle or while you lean against a wall. However, the most effective way to achieve bicycle fit is to have the bicycle bolted in a stationary training device so that you can concentrate on maintaining a realistic position during the adjustments. If you use a wind trainer that leaves the front wheel on when it's bolted in, be sure to put something (a block of wood, etc.) under the front wheel to make sure the contact patches of the tires are on the same plane, or that the axles of both wheels are level with each other before making any adjustments. This will duplicate the true attitude of the bike as it would be ridden on pavement. You shouldn't rely on the top tube of the bike as your measure of level because many bikes have "sloping top tubes" that angle down from the head tube to an inch or more below the seatpost binder collar of the seat tube. A sloping top tube gives the rider more clearance. In the case of bikes that have suspension forks, it will also show the true attitude of the bike after the initial pre-load sag of the fork is taken up by your body weight, from which a more accurate adjustment of the saddle and stem can be made.

Foot Position

The place to start fitting a bicycle is with the foot. After choosing a pedal retention system, you should ensure that your foot fits squarely on the pedal and that the ball of your foot strikes an imaginary line through the center of the pedal axle. The key is to ensure that your foot is not too far forward or too far behind the center of the pedal.

As you pedal a bicycle the joints of the knees and the rotation of the feet at the ankles is not always in unison. The knee may turn inward as the foot turns out during the pedal stroke, or vice versa. Whether your feet pronate (arches fall inward) or supinate (high arch), or they point outward or inward when you walk, also has an effect on the relation between the knee joint with the foot on the pedal.

The knee joint bends as a door hinge would with little rotational movement, whereas the foot/ankle have rotation in a number of directions, all helping give a certain amount of relief to the static knee joint. When you fix the foot on the pedal (as with cleats) you eliminate, or at least greatly hinder, that movement which can put stress on the knee. If you're using cleated shoes and you notice aching in the knees that wasn't there before, this is probably the reason. Try to adjust the cleat to allow the foot to rest on the pedal at an angle close to that when you walk. If pain persists you probably need to go back to toeclips and straps for awhile: if the aches go away, you know the problem was the foot position on the cleated pedal.

If you do use cleated shoes (Shimano©, Onza©, Time©, or LOOK©, etc.) make sure your toes are pointed forward in a straight position before you tighten the cleats securely to the shoe. Some cleats afford a certain degree of adjustability, permitting the foot to angle in or out at the heel which effectively places less stress on the knee joint. To fine tune the cleats on your shoes to match the natural position of your feet during pedaling, you can have a bike shop mechanic with a 'Fit Kit' make the adjustments. The alignment device on the Fit Kit is called the 'RAD'© (Rotational Adjustment Device), which visually indicates the movement of your feet as you sit on and pedal a stationary bike. Adjustments are then made to the position of the cleat to match the bio-mechanical motion of the leg, knee and foot.

As of this writing, the RAD is capable of aligning most Shimano, Look, and Time cleats. Other brands

Fig. 6.1b. Checking for proper saddle height

Fig. 6.1c. Notice the pelvic rock, this saddle is too high

such as Onza, Ritchie, and the newer Shimanos, already have "float" built in to the pedal to allow for a certain number of degrees of rotation of the foot when clipped into the pedal.

Saddle Height

Saddle height is measured from the center of the bottom bracket spindle to the middle portion of the saddle where the pelvic bone rests. There are several numerical formulas for adjusting your saddle height, though they can be rendered inaccurate by many things. Crank length, different types of shoes, or even thickness of socks can effect these formulas.

Your saddle height is almost the complete length of your leg. The first thing that feels odd about this to riders with little experience is that they cannot touch the ground with their feet when sitting. But you are not supposed to be able to touch the ground with your feet when you're riding, you're supposed to be able to touch the pedals. Riding with a saddle too low or too high will result in injury because the leg is not working at its optimum extension. When saddle height is adjusted correctly, a cyclist will have only a slight bend in the leg when the crankarm is at the bottom of the pedal revolution and the heel is level with the ground. (Fig. 6.1b). For anyone who has one leg shorter than the other, they need to be sure to use the shorter leg to determine your saddle height.

Aside from using the aforementioned formulas to adjust the saddle height, the most common method is to have a friend hold the bike, or put it in a training stand and place your heels on the pedals and pedal backwards. Adjust the saddle height until you can pedal backwards keeping your heels on the pedals without rocking your pelvis from side to side when viewed from the rear. (Fig. 6.1c). When you return the ball of your foot to the pedal, you should have a slight bend in the leg at the bottom of the pedal stroke.

Always allow your legs to grow accustomed to changes in saddle height for at least 50 to100 miles before making another change, especially raising it. Changes to saddle height should be made gradually and in small increments because they can have adverse effects on the knees. Eventually, raising the saddle—after your legs are developed for cycling—may give you a slight increase in power and leg speed, but not until you have a good base of miles established at the old height. This is the single most important adjustment on your bicycle. This adjustment has a direct influence in preventing knee injuries and on how efficiently you deliver power from your legs to the pedals.

Fig. 6.1d. This saddle is too low to allow the legs to extend properly

A saddle that is too high will feel good initially because it is using the same ligaments and muscles and their motion as walking, but it is not efficient in developing the legs for cycling. It can also cause discomfort to the genital area after constant pivoting over the saddle crown, better known as "hot crotch." (Fig. 6.1d).

A saddle that is set too low will not allow the hamstrings, quadriceps and gluteus muscles to fully extend and contract, therefore limiting the power sources available to you to pedal and possibly adding stress to the knees.

Fore and Aft

The next step is to adjust the saddle to the proper fore and aft position. This adjustment is designed to fit the bicycle to the length of your femur bone. Using a string with something on the end to weigh it down, turn the pedals so that they are at the three and nine o'clock position. Put your right leg in the three o'clock position and place the top of the string under your right kneecap. The weight should cause the string to hang in a straight line through the axle of the pedal. If it doesn't, you will need to loosen the bolt under the saddle to make the proper adjustment.

If the string falls in front of the pedal axle, then the saddle must be slid to the rear of the bicycle. If the string falls behind the pedal axle, the saddle must be slid towards the front of the bicycle. When making fore and aft position adjustments, be careful not to change either the tilt or the height of the saddle as one bolt controls all those settings. In addition, most saddles will become higher as they are slid forward on their rails due to the angle of the rail as it is attached to the base of the saddle.

Variations of the fore and aft saddle position garner different benefits to suit a rider's needs. For example, power riders tend to rest in the rearward saddle position so they can leg press the pedals away from them. This position does not provide for fast spinning because the rider is literally behind the bottom bracket spindle and can cause strain on the knees. Sprinters and riders who spin at a high rpm (most efficient use of power) like the saddle positioned forward over the spindle so they can spin faster. However, this position doesn't afford as much leverage as the rearward position when using bigger gears or during climbing.

Saddle Attitude

The seat must also be adjusted for tilt attitude. To a certain extent, this is determined by the preference of the individual. However, having the nose of the saddle pointing down too much will cause you to feel like you've done about two million pushups during the course of an eight-hour ride, having spent all day trying to keep from sliding off the front of the saddle. Conversely, if the nose of the saddle is too high you may experience numbness in the genitals. (Obviously, not a good thing.) The best method for adjusting saddle tilt is to align the nose of the saddle with the top tube, avoiding an upward or downward position. In the correct riding position your body weight should be centered on the saddle with your arms flexed and relaxed. The saddle should be supporting the majority of your body weight. Saddle tilt is controlled by the bolt located under the saddle, which usually requires a 6mm Allen wrench.

Fitting Notes

When making bicycle adjustments make sure you are wearing the clothing you will be riding in to ensure your saddle height is precisely accurate. The thickness or amount of clothing you wear can effect saddle positioning. You should also take a couple of pedal strokes before making the final adjustments. This will move your body into the position it will be in during the course of riding, as opposed to the position you sat down in.

If you share a bike at work, make the proper adjustments to the mount and record the distance from the center of the bottom bracket spindle to the sit portion (the middle) of the seat. Cut a piece of string equal to that length and mark it with a piece of masking tape. Put your name on the tape and put it in the bike bag. Then, when you start your shift, all you have to do is loosen the quick release binder and hold the string from the center of the bottom bracket spindle to the middle of the seat. Stretch the string until it is taut and close the quick release. Bingo, your saddle height is set!

Some people mark their seatposts so they'll know where their saddle height is, but eventually the marks wear off. Also, manufacturers of light weight alloy components caution riders to prevent scarring (as in nicks, deep scratches, "file" marks from marking a seat post height) of these components, as it can cause weakening of the bar or seat tube at that point causing a metal fatigue failure, which could result in serious injury to the rider. Beyond that, you really shouldn't mark an expensive seatpost, especially if it's a company ride.

Seatposts and stems are marked with the maximum limit they can be raised out of the seat or steerer tubes. There must be a sufficient amount of post or stem inside the frame to support the stress and weight. **DO NOT RIDE WITH THE SEATPOST OR STEM EXTENDED BEYOND THAT POINT!** Doing so risks snapping the seat tube or seat post, or causing the stem

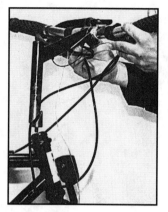

Fig. 6.1e. The handlebar stem

to pop out of the steerer tube. These disasters will undoubtedly occur at the worst possible moment, exposing your most tender parts to what is essentially a device for taking core samples.

Handlebar Height and Stem Length/Rise

Handlebar height and reach (distance from the head tube) are personal preference type settings based on rider comfort and fitness level. With the bar set low you replicate the dilemma of a saddle that's set too high (i.e. body weight biased too far forward causing arm and hand fatigue.) This can also have an effect on you ability to lift the front wheel over obstacles by limiting your leverage and weight transfer to the rear of the bike. The general rule for handlebar height for patrol riding is to achieve a semi-upright riding position, again, putting the weight bias on your butt as opposed to your arms and hands for the long hours of riding. The bar height should be set only after the saddle position is set.

One method of setting the bar height is by raising and lowering the stem in the head tube. The stem is the "L" shaped component that has one end inserted into the steerer tube of the fork (inside the head tube of the frame), with the other end clamping the handlebar. (Fig. 6.1e). A long Allen bolt through the top of the stem is threaded into an alloy "lug" down in the steerer tube. As the bolt is tightened, the lug grabs the side wall of the head tube and secures the stem in that position, preventing it from moving up and down, or side to side, and providing the ability to "steer" the front wheel.

While there is very little height adjustment on most mountain bike stems, you can usually achieve movement of about one inch up or down. The exception to this method is in the case of the newer "threadless" head set/steerer tube type forks where there is no stem bolt holding the stem in position per se. Bar height on the threadless types is only adjustable by changing the stem itself, for one with more or less of the angle (height) you need. This is also a viable method of raising or lowering the bars on a traditional stem set-up.

Stems are made in many different "rises" and lengths, both threadless and threaded, to offer just about any comfort setting a rider could want. Remember that a longer stem does not always correspond to a taller bar height. Likewise, a stem with a higher rise may give you the desired height but not enough reach to keep your knees from hitting your elbows while you pedal.

6.2 GEAR SHIFTING AND USE

It wasn't until the late 1880s that the "drive train" of bicycles included a chain and sprockets like those on modern bicycles. Before that time, the bicycle was either pushed along like a scooter with a seat, or propelled with pedals attached permanently to the front wheel. These fixed pedals resembled the type most often found on today's tricycles. An early bicycle with 26- or 27-inch wheels required the cyclist to pedal very rapidly to travel at even a moderate ground speed. In order to travel at higher speeds, the front wheel, which was pedaled, had to be very large. These big wheeled bikes required great skill to ride and simply weren't practical for many utilitarian uses.

The invention of the chain driven bicycle with chainrings and sprockets allowed the bicycle to use a smaller frame and wheels. By using smaller wheels, but changing the number of teeth on the front and rear sprockets, the rider could essentially create the same effect of a larger wheel. The bike could go faster over flat ground with much less effort for the cyclist. Today's multi-speed bikes work on the same principle. Each different gear combination simulates the effect of larger or smaller wheels. Large (high) gears mimic large-sized wheels, allowing the cyclist to ride faster and longer while pedaling moderately. Smaller (lower) gears simulate the effect of smaller wheels, enabling the rider to pedal up hills, into headwinds and over different surfaces with less effort.

A method was finally devised in the 1930s to change gears while riding. There are several kinds of gear systems, but the type of multi-speed gear system found on most modern bikes, and virtually all mountain bikes, is the derailleur system. The drive train of a derailleur bike consists of several components:

- The chain
- The crankset (pedals, crankarms and chainrings).
- The freewheel (a cluster of gear cogs at the rear axle).
- The derailleurs
- The thumb shifters, Rapid Fire shifters, or Grip Shifts.

The key component in the drive train is the derailleur system. Small mechanical arms on derailleurs move the chain from side to side and "derail" it onto a different freewheel cog or chainring. Mountain bikes, like most multi-speed bikes, have two derailleurs, one at the crankset and one for the freewheel. Though the derailleurs can be moved while the bike is stationary or coasting, they can't derail the chain. The chain wheel must be moving forward for a tooth to catch the chain and the shift to take place. With a derailleur pushing it sideways and the chain wheel forward, the chain is grabbed by another cog. Therefore, you must be pedaling in order to change gears.

To determine the number of "speeds" a derailleur-equipped bicycle has, count the number of teeth on the rear freewheel and multiply it by the number of chainrings on the crankset. Most mountain bikes have either 18, 21, or 24 speeds. But calling a bike a "21 speed," is really a misnomer. In reality, many of the gear ratios created are duplicated by other gear combinations. A 21-speed bike may only have 14 or 15 unique gear ratios. The reason mountain bikes have so many gear combinations is to allow a wide range of gears and to minimize the need to shift the front derailleur. Modern derailleur systems use "indexed shifting." Indexed shifting means that moving the shifter, or pushing the shifter button, moves the derailleur a precise, preset distance to the cog desired. One "click" moves it one cog; two "clicks" move it two cogs; and so on. The old style "friction shift" systems require the cyclist to move the shift lever until the desired cog is reached. Friction shifters are much less precise and don't always align the center of the chain on the cog. The cyclist may have to feather the shift lever back and forth subtly until the chain and cog are correctly and quietly aligned.

The Rear Derailleur

"Spinning" is the name given to the style of riding where the cyclist maintains a pedaling cadence with a high number of revolutions per minute. As you become more accustomed to spinning you will find that you are frequently shifting the rear derailleur to attain the gear that allows you to spin comfortably. Your goal should be low pedal force and a higher pedal speed. In order to maintain a fast cadence, an officer must be in a gear that is low enough to allow him to do so. Be cautioned that too low a gear and too low a pedal force will result in your merely "pedaling air." Power is generated two ways in cycling: 1) by pedaling in a higher gear and using sheer muscle power, or 2) by pedaling in a lower gear at a higher cadence. It is possible to pedal at a fast cadence for a long period of time. This is the technique used by racers and long distance riders. Pedaling in too high a gear, on the other hand, will cause the rider to fatigue very quickly and may result in knee injuries. When riding for speed or distance it's important that you learn to choose a gear that allows you to pedal at a target cadence of 75-100 rpm. Obviously, if you are using the bike at slower speeds, for patrol work, or over rugged terrain, you need not try to spin. While riding, changes such as hills, wind or surface texture (e.g., hard surface changing to soft) may require changing gears to adapt. You might find when riding in rough, sandy, or slippery conditions that selecting a higher gear and simply "powering through" may be the best method to choose. Using the rear derailleur to select a different freewheel cog will quickly and easily provide the small changes necessary.

One of the most common mistakes novice cyclists make is their failure to downshift before coming to a stop or when slowing down. If you fail to downshift, you will find you will start out in a gear that is too high to be either comfortable or efficient. Don't let your habits as a motor vehicle driver confuse you. Motor vehicles can be downshifted while stationary—bicycles cannot. Down shift as you are pedaling toward a stop sign or planned stop. But remember, the subtle sound of a downshift may alert suspects you are approaching. There may be times when downshifting before stopping may not be advisable.

The movements of the chain as it goes from one freewheel cog to another are very small and are made very quickly. This is especially true with indexed systems. Most mountain bikes today have 6, 7, or 8 cogs on their freewheels. This gives you a wide range of gears to chose from without having to move the front derailleur. Unless you are concerned about using your gears in precise ascending order (1st, 2nd, and 3rd, etc.), frequent changes of chainrings should not be necessary.

The Front Derailleur

Mountain bikes have three chainrings attached to the crankset. This is called a triple crankset. The front derailleur has to move the chain from one chainring to another. Officers riding on smooth, level surfaces will soon discover they will rarely need the smallest chainring. This small ring, often called a "granny gear," is for exceptionally low gearing and is usually used for steep hills and certain off-road conditions. Most police riding is done using the middle chainring. This includes riding at slow speeds and in most urban settings. The big chainring, sometimes called the "road gear," is usually saved for those times when speed is what you want!

Front derailleurs do not shift as precisely or quickly as the rear derailleur. It may occasionally rub noisily on the chain. This usually happens when the chain is angled and is on either the largest or the smallest freewheel cog. When this occurs the officer will hear a scraping or rubbing sound while pedaling. If you are trying to move quietly around an area, it is especially annoying! "Feathering" the front derailleur slightly away from the chain should eliminate the offensive noise. This may not be possible if the front derailleur is a totally preset indexed system. Some indexed systems make allowances for this problem and have a little "play" in the front shifter for making subtle movements to correct the scraping problem.

Derailleurs can also go out of adjustment and move the chain completely off the chainrings or freewheel to either the inside or the outside. This may require you to stop and remount the chain. Front derailleurs can often be remounted while pedaling and shifting. Because of the greater number of mid-range cogs on the freewheel, as opposed to the crankset, the chain is much less likely to be thrown off by the rear derailleur. The precision of indexed systems also makes it less likely the chain will be thrown completely off the freewheel.

6.3 PROPER BRAKING TECHNIQUE

L earning how stop a bicycle effectively should be second only to learning how to balance. Of all the skills a cyclist has, the ability to use one's brakes to their fullest advantage is a most valuable asset.

The brakes that are found on today's high-quality bicycles are extremely efficient. It doesn't really matter if they're single pivot side pull, dual pivot side pull,

U brake, or cantilever, they can all stop on a dime using the proper technique.

The myth that merely touching the front brake will bolt you over the handlebars is completely untrue. Only a combination of mistakes can throw you over the handlebars while using the front brake. When a motorist stops at a red light, he doesn't engage the front and rear brakes separately and neither should a cyclist. The front brake on any vehicle, whether it's a car, motorcycle, or bicycle is more efficient because of weight transfer. However, using the front and rear brakes in unison will reduce stopping distances dramatically.

Following the principle that for every action there is an equal and opposite reaction, we can understand how the front brake wields so much power. When you apply either the front or rear brake, the bicycle begins to slow and your weight transfers forward because of inertia. With weight on the front wheel when it is braked, there is more contact with the road, making braking more effective. If you apply the rear brake forcefully enough, the rear wheel will skid. This is because your weight and the weight of the bicycle have transferred forward and lofted the rear wheel, rendering that brake useless. A wheel that is skidding during the braking process is completely useless. You have no control over a locked wheel and its drag coefficient is only slightly higher than a wheel that is rolling.

There are two types of braking actions: planned and unplanned. Planned braking would include stopping for a stop sign, speed reduction prior to or just after a turn, or anytime you know you need to slow down or stop well in advance of having to do so.

Unplanned braking is the immediate need to reduce speed as rapidly as possible because of a previously unknown or unforeseen obstacle or condition.

When riding at a moderate speed, using planned braking, you can use both the front and rear brakes to stop without making any adjustments to your body position. The key to this process is to apply both brakes evenly and smoothly. This sounds very simple, and it is. There are some conditions that exist during planned braking you should pay special attention to:

1. **Brake before and after turns, not while in the turn itself.** The tire's contact with the road is minimal while you're in the turn, and braking increases your chances of having the bike slip out from underneath you. Always try to remain as upright as possible while braking, especially during wet conditions.

2. **Try to steer towards a clean portion of the pavement before beginning to brake.** Braking ability is reduced greatly if you are on a loose surface. Such things as gravel, road debris, oil, or even water can make a big difference in how long it takes you to stop.

3. **Apply the brakes in wet weather prior to the time that you need them.** Give the pads and rims a few revolutions to dry them off. This will enable braking to occur as it normally would.

There will be times when you will need to apply the brakes while pedaling. A couple examples would be, making a U-turn in a tight space or riding through an area crowded with pedestrians. When a car makes a U-turn, the driver is not saddled with the responsibility of staying upright against the force of gravity.

When riding a bicycle, your tools against gravity are power and momentum. If you don't apply power to the pedals during a tight U-turn, the front wheel, which has been turned drastically to one side, will cause the bicycle to lose momentum. Once momentum is lost, only luck or extreme skill will keep you upright.

If you apply the rear brake lightly but continuously and pedal slowly through the U-turn, the bicycle will almost balance itself. Use only the rear brake in this instance. Normally, the bicycle is leaned, not steered.

A tight U-turn at slow speed is a pure steering experience. Using the front brake while the front wheel is at a near 90-degree angle will cause the bicycle to stall.

When patrolling areas crowded with pedestrians, use light but continuous pressure on the front and rear brakes while pedaling slowly for maximum low-speed control. In both of these braking-under-power circumstances, use a low gear so you can make small speed adjustments.

The panic stop is a good example of unplanned braking. Just as the name implies, the goal is to get to 0 mph in a hurry. Unplanned braking requires the use of your eyes, brain, and body. The element of danger that exists between planned and unplanned braking is the fact that someone else selected your braking circumstance without your prior knowledge.

Use your eyes to search for possible conflicts with cars, pedestrians, and road conditions or hazards. Once you have visually identified a possible conflict, summarize in your mind the many ways this unplanned condition could affect you. Here's an example:

You are approaching an intersection, which you intend to cross when a car passes you on the left. The car could continue straight through the intersection and not produce any problems for you at all. The car could make an immediate right-hand turn after passing and force you to turn with it or make a panic stop. The car could pass you, then pull immediately to the curb with the brakes on to get a parking space, requiring a panic stop.

You can make an educated guess as to what a driver may do by looking at their actions. For instance, what is the driver looking at? If he or she appears to be concentrating on the traffic to the left, chances are they will make a right turn in front of you. Once you identify a possible conflict and formulate an escape plan, you waste little time being shocked and immediately react to the situation.

Now that you know how to incorporate your eyes and brain into the braking process it's time to cover physical attributes of the panic stop. The key to effective stopping is weight transfer. When you reduce speed with the brakes, your weight transfers forward. To reduce the chance of pitch-over you must transfer your weight towards the rear of the bicycle prior to aggressive braking. Pitch-over, occurs when your center of gravity moves toward the stem and handlebars of the bicycle. If you are sitting in the seat while making a medium speed panic stop, your weight will transfer forward to the front of the bicycle. If you increase your speed or aggressiveness with the brake levers while remaining in the seat, your weight will transfer farther forward on the bicycle and your body will be thrown forward.

Fig. 6.3a. Proper panic braking technique

Knowing how weight transfer works will help you understand why the front brake is more effective than the rear. Practice the following formula during unplanned or panic stops:

Start by placing the pedals in the 3 o'clock and 9 o'clock positions (horizontal to the ground). (Fig. 6.3a). Thrust your buttocks out of the seat and over the rear axle. When transferring your weight to the rear of the bicycle, keep in mind that you want your buttocks to go straight back, not higher than the seat and not lower. This starts the forward transfer of your weight from well behind the saddle and makes pitch-over almost impossible. But don't expect to make a series of mistakes and get away without laying down some skin.

After transferring your weight over the rear axle you grasp the front and rear brakes firmly. Be sure to use only your index and middle fingers on the brake levers. This enables you to keep your thumb, ring and little fingers on the handlebars to remain in complete steering control during the braking action. With so few fingers on the brake lever you are also able to make minute adjustments in brake lever pressure. With four fingers on the lever, it's usually all or nothing—neither of which is very effective.

Apply the front brake a little harder than the rear, because the front brake is the most effective. If the rear wheel starts to skid this means your weight has transferred forward a sufficient distance to loft the rear wheel. Slightly reduce pressure on the front brake lever until the rear wheel stops skidding. This process reduces the forward weight transfer and gives you the maximum amount of braking power that your brakes have to offer without risk. If you choose to ignore the sound of a skidding rear tire while both brakes are engaged, you can expect a trip to the pavement.

Once the bicycle is stopped, slide your buttocks forward until you are over the top tube of the bicycle frame. At this point, you should be intimately familiar with whatever pedal retention system you are using so you can put a foot down to balance. Granted, falling over because your feet are trapped in the pedals isn't going to hurt like hitting a car or a brick wall, but it is embarrassing.

A pedal retention system that does not incorporate the use of the hands to gain release is ideal for unplanned braking. Toe clips and straps can also be used but they must be loose enough so you can extract your foot without using your hands.

Elements of A Panic Stop

Practice these important steps to improve your panic stop:

1. Place pedals in the 3 & 9 o'clock position.
2. Thrust buttocks off the seat and over the rear axle. When your buttocks are over the rear axle make sure you don't break the seat plane. Strive to get your weight as far back as possible; this will allow you to stop very rapidly.
3. Apply the front and rear brakes with the index and middle fingers only, while ensuring the front brake is engaged a little harder than the rear.

5. Slide forward over the top tube of the frame and put a foot down to balance.

It's almost impossible to take a trip over the handlebars when you use the proper technique -- unless you start with a bad position.

For example, if you were descending a steep hill and didn't push your buttocks back as far as you could, you could easily be launched over the handlebars. This is because the bad position is magnified by two factors: the hill's forward transfer of your weight and the braking action. To avoid this, make sure your weight is thrust as far back as possible and reduce pressure on the front brake when the rear wheel starts to skid.

Another special circumstance would be, if you were required to make a panic stop on flat terrain with numerous potholes. Allowing your front wheel to drop into a hole of any size will increase the forward weight transfer. Depending on your speed and the depth of the hole you could be sent over the handlebars. Under these circumstances, you can avoid a launch by steering around any obstacle that would increase your forward weight transfer while braking.

As with all rules, there are exceptions. Descending a set of stairs is not a bad time to use the front brake. Actually it's about the only help you have on long stair descents. Although it seems like the front wheel would "dig in" as soon as you touched the front brake, this is not true. If you have your weight moved toward the rear axle, gravity will allow your front wheel to float over the steps instead of digging in. One of the chief reasons for this is that the front wheel never really touches the flat portion of the stair treads. Usually during stair descents, both the front and rear wheels are riding edges of the steps as opposed to the flat portions we use when walking up or down them.

These circumstances are not meant to be a complete listing of what can or can't go wrong during unplanned braking. Usually there are a million ways to do something wrong and only a couple of ways to do it right. Good common sense, clear thinking, and proper technique are your best defense against the many unplanned obstacles that might arise.

Training Exercises

Following is a list of training exercises that will help you and the members of your unit develop good braking technique.

Before you begin, select a site that is similar to your normal riding conditions, such as concrete, asphalt, or brick. Ideally, if you can block a road that is lightly traveled, you will have a realistic setting. If a parking lot is used, make sure that it has not been recently paved. Fresh blacktop is very slick, especially when it's wet. Make sure the area is free of traffic so you can concentrate solely on braking technique.

1. Before teaching anyone to brake properly, especially police officers, you must demonstrate that your principles work. Set up a braking lane with traffic cones in front of your students. Explain that you will not apply the brakes until you reach the first cone of the braking lane. Use a hand-held speed measuring device or a bicycle computer to verify that your 15 mph testing speed is constant.

   From a normal riding speed of 15 mph, demonstrate how long it takes to stop using only the rear brake, while remaining in the seat. Next, use both the front and rear brakes from 15 mph while remaining in the seat and allow the students to measure the difference in the two stopping distances. After that, show the students a panic stop using only the front brake. In this demonstration you can usually exceed the 15 mph speed and still stop sooner than you did using only the rear brake. Having your weight shifted over the axle is extremely important in this exercise.

2. After the demonstrations, break the class into small groups and pair each with an instructor. Set up a 60-foot braking lane for each group and have the students practice planned braking. Braking should begin at the first cone in each lane. Repeat this exercise several times.

   While continuing to use the first cone in the braking lane as the signal to start braking, have the students practice panic stops. After they have become familiar with the panic stop, switch the signal to begin braking to a verbal command given by the instructor. In this exercise, each student should ride in the braking lane at 15 mph until the instructor yells "brake." The student then immediately executes a panic stop. Be sure the braking lanes are far enough apart so the students do not become confused and brake on another instructor's command. The instructor should also note each student's position in the lane when the command to brake was given. This is so measurements of the stopping distance can be taken, and the students can see their progress.

3. Next, wet the students' bike rims with a hose or a water-filled fire extinguisher, and have them do some planned braking. After they've experienced the effects of water on the rims, wet down both the braking lanes and the rims. Have the students do these exercises very slowly at first, then bring them up to normal riding speeds.

   Save the braking-under-power exercises for last. Towards the end of the day the students attention span gets very short. These exercises present little danger to the student, even if they haven't been paying close attention to the instructor.

4. The next exercise involves the practice of U-turns. Start by having the students make U-turns without the confines of cones. After they have mastered this, create a lane of cones and have the students per-

form U-turns inside the lane. As the students become more proficient, narrow the lane until they can no longer perform a U-turn. A contest to see which student can make the tightest U-turn will add spice to this exercise.

5. Students should now be ready for the pedestrian exercise. To begin, place traffic cones intermittently in a lane 8-feet wide and 60-feet long. The object of this exercise is to spend as much time as possible riding in the lane, while successfully dodging the cones which represent pedestrians. Five seconds is deducted from a rider's time if they put a foot down and 10 seconds is deducted if they hit a pedestrian. Remember, the object is to see how long the rider can stay in the pedestrian lane. With any of these exercises, remember: Never challenge students to go beyond their capabilities when injury could occur.

These exercises are just a few of the many ways to practice effective braking. This text is meant to be a good foundation to get you started and is by no means the end all to good braking technique. Practice every chance you get, and allow no one to plan your future.

6.4 BICYCLE HANDLING TECHNIQUES

B asic riding skills are essential to successful and efficient police bike patrol and will enable you to work more effectively and safely in varying terrain situations and across various obstacles.

These riding techniques will be used daily. Practice these basics as often as possible; do not rely on duty time to perfect your skills. Pick a place where vehicular traffic won't impede or make your session hazardous. For some of the drills, you may want to use a grass covered area, to lessen the chance of road rash injuries in the event of a fall.

Arguably, there is no better way to hone bike handling skills, such as obstacle clearing, hill climbing and descending, than off-road riding. A single track, as it's called, will sharpen your balance and steering abilities. Rock strewn and root-lined hills will test all of your bike handling know-how. While there are efforts to close many mountain bike trails, you can probably find some in or near your town worth riding for the experience. Contact your local cycling clubs or shops for help in finding them, and abide by the rules of the trail.

While off-road riding can shape your handling skills, one of the best ways to develop stamina and endurance is on a road bike. Paved roads allow you to work on your hill climbing ability, while offering the opportunity to concentrate more on expending energy to increase endurance and building leg power for sprints. A road bike allows faster acceleration and higher sustained speeds for a better overall aerobic workout. If you can't find a road bike to use, you can get an equivalent workout by putting some slick tires on your mountain bike to get a smoother ride with a little less rolling resistance.

A Word About Practice

Many bike patrol officers around the country are not cyclists in their off-duty time. Some rely solely on their duty-time riding to stay fit and able to operate the bike skillfully. This will hopefully wane as IPMBA education efforts reach the thousands of police cyclists on the street and the hundreds who emerge every month around the country. Time should be set aside by your agency for the bike patrol to train as a unit or in small groups on at least a monthly basis.

Patrolling by bicycle requires total dedication to the craft and a commitment to maintaining the highest physical capabilities. This is not solely for your own benefit, but also for that of other officers who may be relying on your ability to sprint to their aid and have some strength left to help make an arrest or end a fight.

In pursuit of that commitment, it's a good idea for bike officers to develop and maintain a regular aerobic exercise and strength training regimen, in addition to good nutritional habits. Furthermore, officers should read as much about cycling and accompanying equipment as possible. After all, the bike is a tool of your trade. Practice everything you know about bike patrol often. Use uncommitted patrol time on duty if possible, but certainly don't rely on that alone.

Dismounts

Bike patrol officers will frequently come across suspects and suspicious people while riding their bikes. Officer safety requires officers to dismount before they conduct field interviews or otherwise confront such people. Officers cannot safely control, handcuff, or fight a person with a bicycle between their legs! Bike officers must consequently know how to dismount quickly and safely while keeping the suspect in sight at all times. Dismounting skills must be developed to the point that they become second nature to the cycling police officer.

The dismount should take place before contacting the suspect, if possible. Techniques that require the officer to physically contact the suspect with his bike before dismounting may look dramatic, but they often knock the officer off balance too, placing him at risk of injury, assault or embarrassment. Such techniques also may fall outside departmental use of force guidelines. It is strongly recommended that these techniques be avoided.

Crossover Dismount

The simplest, and therefore most effective, dismount is the crossover dismount. The first action the cyclist must take with any dismount is to disengage any pedal retention system in use. Some officers will totally remove their foot and let the toe clip or strap hang upside down beneath their pedal. Depending on the device used, this can cause a scraping sound on the ground that may eliminate any stealth advantage. Others will pull their foot out of the toe clip or strap and place their toes on the back edge of the pedal cage for easy exit. Others may try to leave their toe clip straps loose so they may rapidly enter and exit the device. The foot will twist when exiting, causing a loose strap to tighten firmly enough to hold the foot in place, if it isn't already partially out of the toe clip. If the foot becomes trapped in the toe clip, it will likely cause a sudden and painful fall. Every time officers exit their bikes they should make a conscious effort to remove the pedal retention system as they would when approaching a suspect. Officers can develop this skill to be instinctive by doing a crossover dismount each time they exit their bike.

The next step in a crossover dismount is the maneuver that gives it its name. The cyclist crosses one leg behind the saddle and over the back wheel, resting it against the other leg. The cyclist then comes to a stop with both legs on the same side of the bike. People have a "dominant" or strong side and most have more control standing on the left side of the bike. It's important that the officer be able to exit off of either side of the bike. The position of the suspect against a building or other object may make a left-side exit impractical or unsafe.

When exiting the bike, step off with the back or dangling foot first. Then, while still gripping the handlebar for balance, carefully remove the remaining foot from the pedal. Once both feet are on the ground and the officer is balanced, the bike can be released. Many officers choose to place the bike down carefully on its left side so the rear derailleur doesn't contact the ground and get damaged or knocked out of adjustment. In a pursuit or high-risk situation, however, the bike may just fall to the ground unpredictably. You may want to practice placing the bike quietly. When exiting the bike, leave it resting some distance away from the actual contact, perhaps 8- to 10-feet away. The officer doesn't want the bike underfoot if the subject resists and a physical confrontation ensues. There is no part of a bike an officer wants to fall on or trip over during a fight.

Rolling Crossover Dismount

The rolling dismount is one of the most effective exiting maneuvers, because it enables the officer to immediately walk or run upon dismount. This maneuver is often used to apprehend fleeing suspects, or achieve various tactical deployments from the bike. It requires a good sense of balance and, as with most hand-eye-coordination skills, some mental preparation.

It is a good idea to prepare for the dismount by visualizing where and how you will actually leave the bike. With some practice, this mental preparation will narrow to a second or two, and eventually the maneuver will become reflexive. Initially, it is advisable to practice at a slower speed, working up to higher speed dismounts.

If your bike is equipped with toe clips and straps on the pedals (or some other means of foot retention), it may be safer to use the underside of the pedals or disregard the retention devices until you're comfortable getting off and away from the bike. Some officers do this even after mastering the move as an added safety precaution.

Next, you must decide which side of the bike will be most advantageous for you to dismount from, based on the reason for dismounting or the particular situation you are about to encounter. Depending on the situation, you will either lay the bike down or use the kickstand. Dismounting from the left side of the bike is preferred, especially for practice, for the following reasons:

1. The kickstand is usually mounted on the left side.
2. Dismounting from the right side can be hazardous due to the location of the chainrings that can cause injury in a mishap (especially to the Achilles tendon).
3. Laying the bike down on the derailleur side (right side) can cause damage to vital components, especially at higher speeds.

The dismount can be initiated at any speed but you will need to be able to keep up the same speed and momentum (running or walking) as the bike when you decide to step off. Again, mental preparation is a factor.

Begin the maneuver with both hands on the handlebars, and the brake levers engaged by at least the index and middle fingers of both hands. Look at the place you want to stop the bike, not at the ground in front of the wheel. Once you've decided which side of the bike you're getting off, shift to a gear that will be easy to start off in after you've stopped, and move the pedal on that side of the bike to the down position.

Fig. 6.4a. Swinging the leg over the rear of the bike, preparing to dismount

Next, swing the other leg back over the saddle and the rear of the bike. (Fig. 6.4a). This will put you in a standing position on the pedal in the six o'clock position. The leg you've swung over the bike is the "trailing leg" and, in most cases, will be the one that touches down first. (Fig. 6.4b). You will want to keep it close to the forward leg because positioning it too far back can create balance problems (especially at higher speeds) and may cause you to do a split when you touch down. This usually results in a fall.

Fig. 6.4b. Touching down with trail leg

As you stand on the down pedal, your body weight should be centered over the bottom bracket along the seat tube, with the bike in an up-right position. The bike should not be leaning left or right and, ideally, your head and shoulders should be in line with the top tube. Don't lean your body across the frame to the opposite side of the bike to try to maintain balance, you may quickly reach the point of no return and wind up on the ground on top of the bike.

At this point, it's time to make your speed and braking decisions. It is crucial to the success of this maneuver—and your own well being—that you control the braking with a bias toward the rear brake. If you use too much front brake, your weight will shift forward (over the front wheel) as you stop. The momentum will either send you over the handlebars with the bike tumbling after you, or cause you to trip over your forward leg after you step off the bike with the trailing leg. (If you've positioned your body weight over the bottom bracket and seat tube, your fore/aft balance should be just right). Gradually begin to apply the brakes equally, using

Fig. 6.4c. Laying the bike down on the left side

the amount of pressure necessary to affect the stop at the speed desired, while maintaining fore and aft balance.

Remember to keep your eyes on the place where you intend to dismount. Don't look at the front wheel, your feet, or the ground beneath the bike; it throws off your equilibrium and impairs your ability to safely control the bike from this standing position. Once you've mastered the hand-eye-body coordination of this move and it has become instinctive, you can shift your focus to the person you are stopping to contact. With practice you can do these dismounts while keeping your eyes on the suspect, and not have to look at you bike. Your kickstand will always be in the same place. Teach your foot to remember where the kickstand is, so your eyes can watch the suspect. Suspects are generally less predictable than kickstands. When you have reached the speed at which you feel safe to dismount, apply the brakes harder to bring the bike to as complete a stop as possible. If you are traveling at a high speed, the bike may begin to skid (especially on loose footing), so don't step off until you feel that you can keep up with the momentum of the bike as it continues to move. If you're using toe clips/straps, it is extremely important to be sure that you can get your foot out of the toe strap before you decide to get off.

You will normally step off with the trailing leg first and then the foot that was on the pedal, because at lower speeds it causes less disruption of balance than just hopping off with both feet at the same time. Then, either lay the bike down or deploy the kickstand.

If you dismount from the left side of the bike while moving and intend to lay it down, it is helpful to let go of the left side of the handlebar first (releasing the front brake lever) while laying the bike down. The right hand should be locking the rear brake and lowering the bike to the ground at the same time. (Fig. 6.4c). This gives you control of where the bike goes, preventing it from bouncing up and hitting you from behind, and in some cases minimizing the potential for damage. Obviously this will not work if you lay it down from the right side because you would be locking the brake of the front wheel, which probably isn't touching the ground. There may be situations (as in dismounting from a standing position on the bottom bracket shell) where you will let the bike go its own way after you get off. Otherwise, deploy the kickstand making sure it has a solid footing.

Bottom Bracket Dismount

An alternate version of the rolling dismount is to "launch" from a standing position on the bottom bracket shell. This maneuver should only be used for a suspect take-down, and its inherent risks should be considered before using it. Those risks include: 1)slipping at the point of departure from the bike; 2) landing on your face; 3) getting off too soon and not being able to keep up with the momentum; and 4) since you are pushing off the bike as opposed to laying it down, you have no real control over where it goes and what or who it may hit.

Fig. 6.4d. Preparing for bottom bracket dismount

The bottom bracket dismount begins the same as the rolling dismount, but the trailing leg is positioned on top off the bottom bracket shell where it meets the seat and down tubes. (Fig. 6.4d). When it's time to get off the bike you push off the bike with both feet simultaneously, while letting go of the handlebars. You may do this to get into running mode from the bike, but that means you've given up on your mechanical advantage over a suspect. You'll probably be further away from your bike than in a regular rolling dismount because you've let it roll away uncontrolled. It, therefore, makes sense to use it only when you're as close to the suspect as possible and are attempting to launch yourself directly onto the person's back for the take-down.

To practice this maneuver without too much concern for broken bike parts, get an old beaten up bike out of the impound yard and practice on a grassy area to minimize injury to you and the equipment. If you must use your own bike or a department issue bike, do the maneuver at slower speeds to lessen the impact and bike momentum.

Rear Wheel (Power) Slide

The rear wheel slide, or "hook-slide" as it is commonly called, is used to enable the officer to change direction and dismount quickly. It is a basic component of several two officer contact maneuvers.

This maneuver is done while moving and is sometimes used to make quick face-to-face contact with suspects, before they have a chance to think about making an evasive move. In this scenario, the officer should pick an area to make the stop, leaving enough room to make a swinging arc of a turn toward, but well ahead of, the suspect. This creates a safety zone between you and the bike in case you have to back up while on foot.

Before reaching the point where the slide will occur, you will need to decide which side of the bike you should dismount from and stand on the opposite pedal (the outside pedal), with your butt off the saddle and straddling the top tube. Remember, you're standing on the outside pedal that will be on the "up side" of the bike after you lay it over. Pay attention to this as it is the opposite of the setup for the rolling dismount. Be mentally prepared to make the move; visualize yourself doing the maneuver before you commit.

As you stand on the "outside" pedal, your body weight should be biased toward the front of the bike and supported mainly by the outer leg. This is necessary to lighten the rear of the bike to cause the locked wheel to skid. If you have too much of your body weight over the rear wheel, it will not skid. The basic tenets of braking, as taught in the IPMBA Police Cyclist Course, are that an unweighted wheel will skid as opposed to a weighted wheel which will gain traction. Therefore, if you have too much weight on the rear wheel when you try to make it slide with the bike leaned into a turn (as in this maneuver), the tire will grab the pavement and the momentum will send you over the bike in the direction you were initially headed -- not the direction you chose to turn. In motorcycle road racing this is called getting "high-sided," and it can be hazardous to your health.

When you reach the point where you want to make the turn back toward the suspect and dismount, lean the bike in that direction and counter-steer with the handlebars (turn them in the opposite direction of where you want to go). This will assist in laying the bike down against its forward momentum. It may be helpful to lean the inside of the thigh of the "outside," weight-supporting leg against the top tube for leverage. Simultaneously, you will plant the inside foot as your pivot point for the turn/slide, and lock up the rear brake. (Fig. 6.4e). Only practice will help you determine how far from the bike to plant your pivot foot. It must be far enough away to help lean the bike; but not so far that it causes you to lose balance as you try to step off the bike. (Fig. 6.4f).

Locking the rear brake will cause the rear tire to slide in the direction you were going before you turned the bike. As the rear wheel slides away from you, you will be laying the bike down so you can step off and away, unencumbered by the bike. (Fig. 6.4g). If you dismount from the left side of the bike, you should try to employ the same handlebar control as the rolling dismount: release the front brake first, and so on.

If you find that you're having trouble getting the bike to turn and lean over, try more counter-steering and pressure on the top tube with the outer leg. If the rear wheel doesn't slide, you probably have too much weight over it. Correct this by moving your weight forward. (A good rule of thumb is to have your head and shoulders above or over the handlebars). Remember, this maneuver must be done with some speed. The rear wheel needs momentum to slide. It won't work at a

Fig. 6.4e. Planting the inside foot and locking the rear brake for a power slide

Fig. 6.4f. Pivoting off of the inside foot as rear wheel skids

Fig. 6.4g. Almost stopped

Fig. 6.5a. Pedalling through from 1 o'clock position as front wheel clears obstacle

Fig. 6.5b. Unweighting the rear wheel

walking pace. (Again, if you are new at this, practice on grassy areas until you get it down.)

6.5 OBSTACLE CLEARING

The ability of mountain bike police officers to get up and over small obstacles found in the urban environment is one of the many advantages the mountain bike provides. Curbs, stairs, parking blocks, and medians are common obstacles bike police encounter daily. The mountain bike, with its versatility and durability, makes it easy for bike patrol officers to go just about anywhere. To do so, however, they must have a good understanding of the necessary body position and bike handling skills.

The body position used for ascending and descending obstacles is similar to that described previously in panic stops. The knees and elbows are bent for shock absorption and the weight is back on the saddle to place more weight on the back tire. The position of the pedals will depend upon which maneuver is being performed.

Curb Hopping

The most frequent obstacle most bike officers in urban areas confront are curbs. The technique used to clear curbs requires proper gear selection, fore and aft body weight distribution and some upper body strength.

The best way to approach and clear a curb or like obstacle, is from a perpendicular angle. In preparation for the move you should shift to a gear that will allow you to pedal through the maneuver after the front wheel has cleared the obstacle, and rotate one of the pedals to the one o'clock position (usually your stronger or "power" leg).

Next, get off the saddle and shift your weight down onto the handlebars to compress either the front tire or, if so equipped, your suspension fork. Once you feel the compression, allow it to rebound back upward, and as it does, pull up and back on the bars and shift your weight toward the back of the bike. Shifting your weight will lighten the front end. (Fig. 6.5a). You don't want the wheel to slam into the curb. At very slow speeds you can "wheelie" it up over the curb using the correct gears and "power pedal" technique.

Once the wheel has cleared the curb, shift your weight to the front of the bike and pedal through. If you don't shift your weight forward, the rear wheel will slam into the curb with your body weight as an extra burden. (Fig. 6.5b). The result is usually a bent rim. Again, it is important to have an easy gear, but not too easy or you'll spin the pedals and lose balance. Pre-selecting a gear may not always be possible, as in pursuit situation.

Angular approach curb hop. As it is not always possible to meet a curb with a head-on approach, an angular method can be used to save the time of dismounting or circling around to take a new angle. This method is not as fast as the perpendicular approach but, with practice, is a close second. Practice the following exercise from different angles.

Shift into a gear that will enable you to pedal through the obstacle. Approach the curb with the leg on the outside (the non-curb side) in the down (6 o'clock) position. When you reach the curb, step onto it with the inside foot and lift the front wheel onto the curb. (Fig. 6.5c). At this point, you should be standing with the outside foot on the pedal in the down position, and the inside foot and the front wheel on the curb. You are still at an angle to the curb.

Next, ratchet the outside foot/pedal to the power position, just below 12 o'clock, and, while keeping your weight centered somewhere around the bottom bracket, pedal forward. (Fig. 6.5d). If your weight is too far forward the rear wheel will slide along the edge of the curb until it is at a perpendicular angle. This may also happen if the ground is wet. Of course, if it is too far back, it will be difficult to pedal the back wheel over the obstacle.

Fig. 6.5c. Standing on curb with inside foot and on down pedal with outside pedal while performing angular curb hop

Fig. 6.5d. Clearing the curb with rear wheel while pedaling forward from 1 o'clock position

Once you pedal off with the outside foot and you feel some forward momentum and the rear wheel clear the curb, get the inside foot on the pedal and continue pedaling through until your balance is secure. Don't worry about getting the inside foot into a toe clip right away, use the back of the pedal until you regain balance.

The most common error in practicing this technique is forgetting which foot to put in the down position on approach. Failing to ratchet the outside pedal up and improper gear selection are also common mistakes. This maneuver requires careful timing and practice to be able to do it quickly.

Clearing parking lot blocks, logs, and other obstacles. There are basically two ways to clear these types of obstacles: "bunny-hop" over them, or employ a modified version of the curb hop. The latter is more appropriate for most police mountain bikes because the extra weight we carry hampers the rider's ability to lift both ends of the bike into the air at the same time as required by the bunny hop.

Before hopping this type of obstacle, you should be sure that the bottom bracket is high enough to allow the chainrings some clearance—especially over concrete parking lot blocks—to avoid bending the chainrings or breaking a chain. This may require a ride-by to scope it out before committing yourself. Don't take a chance on going over the handlebars or damaging your equipment and getting stranded.

When you know the bike will clear the obstacle, proceed as in the curb hop. The only difference is, after the front wheel goes over the obstacle, you won't shift your weight as far forward. You will stand on the pedals with your legs bent at the knees acting as shock absorbers and with your arms relaxed. As you feel the rear wheel climbing the block, shift your weight forward a little until it touches down on the other side. As it's coming down the other side of the block, begin to move your weight back to prevent going over the handle-bars, then pedal through.

Fig. 6.5e. Getting the front wheel high and past the log

To negotiate an obstacle, such as a log, where your chainrings won't clear, you will need to get the front wheel up high and as far past the center of the log as you can, while putting one pedal in the 1 o'clock power position. (Fig. 6.5e). Also be sure to shift out of the big chainring to avoid damage to the chain, and to allow the chainring's teeth to grab the log and help "pull" you over. As the chainring grabs the log, keep your balance centered over the top tube and allow the front wheel to slowly gravitate down to the ground. (Fig. 6.5f). At this point, you will probably have the non-power position foot on the log to maintain balance. Shift your weight back and try to pedal and rock the bike forward at the same time. (Fig. 6.5g). (Obviously, if you didn't clear the center of the log with the chainring, this is going to be difficult.)

Fig. 6.5f. Balance centered, ride the chainring across the log

As the bike begins to roll forward, the rear wheel will be climbing the back side of the log (increasing the steepness of the descent you're now in), so you will need to move your weight back even further to avoid going over the handlebars. With some luck and good balance you should clear the log.

Fig. 6.5g. Weight shifting to back while rocking bike forward

This is an advanced maneuver and should be practiced only after mastering the other skills in this section. The rider should consider the consequences of this type of maneuver, such as a serious fall and possible injury, as well as damage to the chain ring. In addition, you should probably have a couple of helpers "spot" you on either side of the log to catch you in the event of a fall. Bring some extra chainrings when practicing this maneuver.

The Bunny Hop

The bunny hop requires that you get both wheels in the air at the same time to clear an obstacle. This has to be done "on-the-fly" using speed and momentum. As you near the obstacle, be certain that you have the ability to clear it, as an error in judgment for this type of maneuver can be disastrous.

Once you attain your approach speed, you should be in the standing position with the crankarms parallel to the ground. Just as you arrive at the obstacle, force your body weight down on the pedals to compress the tires. This is somewhat of a jumping motion. As the bike begins to rebound up, pull up on the handlebars and up with your feet simultaneously to lift both ends of the bike (you'll be pulling up against the toe straps with your feet to get the rear of the bike airborne). At the same time the back wheel comes up, thrust the handlebars (and bike) forward and across the obstacle.

As the bike lands, try to keep your body weight balanced fore and aft to land on the rear wheel first. This is ideally how it should be done but, as mentioned earlier, the weight of a fully-equipped police bike makes it hard to do. Practice it with a bike stripped of its equipment using one of those huge car-wash style sponges to hop (wet, so it won't move). Speed bumps are also good to practice with. If you use a foot retention pedal system, you have a great advantage over toe clips and straps for bunny hopping, because you can pull the bike up with your legs.

Climbing Stairs

The very mention of this technique at the beginning of a basic course of instruction sends fear through the hearts of some students, but they have already developed the skills necessary during the obstacle clearing drills.

We are not advocating that a student climb a set of 10 steps. Actually we recommend that, unless you have very advanced skill levels, you should only attempt to climb about 4 steps. Start practicing with two steps (stacked shipping pallets can be used to simulate stairs) and gradually work up to your personal limit. It is also recommended to have spotters on either side of the stairs to break your fall in the event of a mishap. The requisites for the maneuver are; basic obstacle clearing know how, and some upper body strength.

To begin, approach the stairs the same as in a curb hop, remembering to pre-select a gear that will allow you to pedal through the obstacle. (Fig. 6.5h). In this case, usually the middle chainring and the next to largest freewheel cog or, the small chainring and the middle freewheel cog will work. The idea is not to be in too low a gear that will cause you to spin out once on top of the stairs causing imbalance and a fall. Keep up some speed and momentum on your approach as the momentum will help carry you up and over.

Fig. 6.5h. Perpendicular approach as possible with proper gear selection

As you reach the stairs you will power down on one pedal while pulling up the front wheel to clear at least the first two steps. (Fig. 6.5i). This requires your weight to be back off the saddle; otherwise, the front wheel will slam into the stairs instead of carrying you over the top. You will not need your brakes to complete the initial phase of this maneuver, so don't grip them tightly as you may inadvertently lock up a wheel and cause a fall.

Fig. 6.5i. Powering down from 1 o'clock pedal position while pulling up front wheel

When the front wheel has landed, you need to begin to pedal through to bring the rear wheel up the stairs. As the rear wheel begins to climb and the front wheel is on top of the last step, you must gradually shift your weight forward to lighten the back of the bike. (Fig. 6.5j). If you don't, the rear wheel will slam into the next step or two and halt your progress. (Note: tire pressure is an important consideration for this drill. While a lower pressure—35/45 psi—will help the climb, it will also permit "pinch flats" as the rear wheel slams into the first step. Conversely, higher pressures—45/65 psi— cause the rim to absorb most of the shock and the result is usually out-or-round or out-of-true wheels).

Fig. 6.5j. Shifting weight forward and pedaling through

After you've shifted your weight forward, continue to pedal through or up, as it may be. You'll realize the importance of momentum and correct gear selection (for your abilities) with practice. (Fig. 6.5k). If you're us-

Fig. 6.5k. Almost up and still pedaling

6.5l. Pick as near a perpendicular line as possible

6.5m. Notice the chain slap caused by using the small chainring

6.5n. Weight back, knees and elbows slightly flexed

ing pallets for this exercise, you'll need to quickly adopt to the stair descending mode as described below. Again, start with two steps and work up. Students get the biggest boost in bike handling confidence after realizing that they were able to clear 4 steps, and that it really wasn't as hard as it looked.

Descending Stairs

This can be one of the most fun, if not scary, drills you will learn and practice. It can also be one of the most disastrous in terms of injury and should be regarded in that light during practice and especially on the street. Generally, you are not limited to the number of stairs you can descend, as opposed to how many you can climb, with a few exceptions. To master this skill you will need a good sense of balance and brake control, along with steady nerves and mental focus. As with ascending, you should start out descending about 3 or 4 steps and work up to your personal comfort level, using spotters to assist.

The preparation requires knowledge that the stairs are not too steep in relation to their length, which could cause you to go over the front of the bike. Are the stairs wet? Is there loose material on the steps that could cause a fall? Also, know what the ground is like at the bottom. If it's soft, it may cause the front wheel to dig in and stop (sending you over the bars), or if it's wet the front tire could slip and result in a fall. If these are unknowns to you while on duty, it would be advisable to dismount and descend on foot carrying the bike. Know the area you patrol and be familiar with the obstacles you can clear and those you can't.

It is preferable to approach from as perpendicular an angle as possible and continue that line down the stairs. (Fig. 6.5l). (You should refrain from trying to steer the bike once you are committed to the descent). Prior to descending, you will need to shift to the large chainring in front to take up any slack in the chain. (Fig. 6.5m). As the bike bounces from step to step, the chain will whip up and down and eventually bounce off the smaller chainrings onto the bottom bracket shell.

Stand on the pedals with the crankarms in the horizontal position, with legs bent at the knees as shock absorbers, and arms flexed and relaxed. (Fig. 6.5n). Your hands should be gripping the bars firmly with at least two fingers of each hand resting on the brake levers. You will mainly be concerned with modulating the rear brake, as too much front brake will shift your weight forward and send you over the bars, resulting in the infamous "face-plant." Ultimately, you want to feel the bike moving beneath you without bouncing in unison with it. Visualize floating above the bike as it rebounds from step to step.

As you roll down the first step, shift your weight way back off the saddle, but don't give up control of the bike for this position. The longer the flight of stairs, the more speed you will gain and have to control. If you try to pick your way down step-by-step it will be arduous and more difficult to maintain balance than if you control a faster descent with the rear brake. As you descend and pick up speed, the frequency of the oscillations caused by the two wheels hitting the edges of the steps becomes greater and there is a point where the wheels seem to be hitting the edges simultaneously. When you reach that point, the ride becomes much smoother than bucking from one step to the next with both wheels at a slower pace. Work your way up to it though; it's not for the beginner, but it is fun!

When you reach the bottom you'll have to keep your weight back until both wheels are safely on the ground. Remember, that you're in the large chainring, so you'll have to shift to a gear compatible with your speed in order to pedal away.

Climbing Hills

As a bike patrol officer, it is important to learn the skill of climbing hills efficiently with regard to energy expenditure. You must be able to function physically when you reach your destination, especially when encountering a violent situation. The lack of an officer's commitment to staying aerobically conditioned is never more evident than when climbing hills. With the type of equipment most officers ride on duty today (i.e., 21 speeds), it should not be a giant chore to learn proper hill climbing technique, if you have a good base of physical fitness.

There are varying opinions in cycling as to the best way to climb: seated or standing; shift before you meet resistance of the hill or after; stay in a gear until your cadence slows considerably, then down-shift or try to maintain the same cadence and shift gears accordingly. The type of terrain is a big factor as well. The bottom line is to find out what works for you based on your physical capabilities and experience in a given set of circumstances. For instructional purposes, this book will discuss one method that seems to promote the most efficient use of energy, and it works for on- and off-road applications.

One of the main aspects of hill climbing is mental focus. Don't defeat yourself mentally with self-doubt before you've ridden 20 yards up the grade. Visualize yourself cresting the hill. If you need to, break the hill up into small goals to achieve, or strive to spin that gear to a certain landmark along the way before you down shift. Accomplishing smaller goals will have a cumulative effect at the top.

For this method, remain on the saddle instead of standing (standing uses more energy because it uses more muscle groups). You will want to stay relaxed to conserve energy, using a light touch on the bars and letting your legs do the work. Keep your shoulders and arms loose so as not to tighten the chest muscles, which will restrict your breathing. Exhale deeply every couple of breaths, expanding your abdominals to aid in the expansion of the rib cage and lungs. Try to adopt a rhythmic breathing pattern, but avoid short stabbing breaths, which use a lot of energy.

Carry as much momentum going into the hill as you can. With proper gear selection, strive to maintain a cadence of about 75 to 95 rpm. A higher cadence uses too much energy and elevates the breathing rate; a lower cadence doesn't pump blood to the muscles as quickly, allowing lactic acid to build up in the muscles resulting in discomfort and early lockup of the quadriceps. As you meet resistance from the slope of the hill, continue pedaling until you reach the lower end of the cadence range and then down-shift to stay in the zone. Stay in the gear as long as you can maintain the optimum cadence, then down shift. Concentrate on "pedaling in circles" instead of mashing down on the pedals with each stroke. This will allow more muscles, like the glutes and hamstrings, to share the work with the quadriceps.

On very steep climbs, you may want to move forward on the saddle a little and pull back on the bars with your arms for leverage. Bend your torso down a little toward the top tube, but don't get cramped up or you will restrict your breathing. It's okay to bob up and down in sync with your cadence, as long as you are not using a great amount of effort to do so.

For off-road applications, fore and aft weight balance are critical to traction. If you are too far forward, the rear wheel will lose traction, while being too far back will cause the front wheel to lighten up and not track accurately or wheelie. Also, it's important to keep your eyes focused on where you want the bike to go — not down at the front tire or at a rock you want to avoid in the trail. If you stare at an obstacle, it's highly likely you will hit it. But don't look too far ahead and fail to prepare for the trail immediately in your path.

There will be times when you "run out of gears," especially off-road, and you'll have to decide to push on (maybe by standing for power) or dismount and walk to conserve energy. It is a common sight to see pro mountain bike racers dismount and carry their bikes up a steep and rocky climb in an effort to save energy and

6.5o. Good downhill form

to avoid possible injury. In some instances, you may be near the top of the hill and you will want to stand (usually up-shifting a gear first) and power over the top to regain momentum. On a long gradual grade, you may want to get out of the saddle to stretch your legs a little before sitting down again and into your spin. These decisions are based on your own physical capabilities against the terrain.

Hill climbing is a learned skill through many miles of practice. If you stick to the basics it will eventually become a lot easier. Remember, the difference between you and a recreational cyclist is that someone's life may be in your hands at the top of that hill—maybe even your own. Ride.

Descending off-road hills differs slightly from the more relaxed on-road variation. Off-road you need to use the techniques described in the stair descent section of this book, except you will be inputting steering changes to negotiate the terrain on the way down. (Fig. 6.5o). The front brake will be more useful than it is on stairs, and body movements will not disrupt balance as on the straight line stair descent. It is also a good idea to look ahead at where you want to go and not down at the wheel or at obstacles in your path. Again, if you stare at it, you're probably going to hit it.

On-road downhill rides require that you bias the braking slightly to the rear, braking before any turns, not while in them. Body position should be on the saddle with the torso bent over at the waist slightly, arms relaxed and fingers poised on the brake levers. For fast curves, lower your torso toward the top tube and point the inside knee out and into the direction of the turn. The effort is to lower the center of gravity on the frame enabling the centrifugal force to use that weight against the tires where they make contact with the road. (Remember, an unweighted wheel will skid). The inside pedal should be in the up position for ground clearance. You will be applying a small amount of counter-steering here, so the inside arm should be mainly in control of the handlebars, until you straighten up.

Of course, there is a point of no return in your lean angle. Once centrifugal force and lean angle exceed the ability of the tire to adhere to the pavement (coefficient of friction), you begin to slide to the outside of the turn. If you can't correct in time or control the skid, you will go down. Get to know your maximum lean angle by allowing the rear tire to skid out a little at a moderate speed.

Tire pressure is important for road traction also. Very high pressure reduces the size of the "contact patch" where the rubber meets the pavement. Lower pressure enlarges it some, but at the expense of rolling resistance in some cases. Lower pressure is preferable in wet road conditions. However, pressure that is too low on dry pavement can cause a loss of control as the tires "squirm" under the side loads of cornering, and could cause the tires to roll off the rim.

Crashing

Whether in practice or on duty, the inevitable will happen: you will crash or fall off the bike. How you handle it will determine the extent of any injuries you might incur. This is an area many officers neglect to talk about, let alone train for. Training is relatively simple: practice falling from the bike to each side and off the front and back. Find an area with soft ground and use an old bike, so you don't have to worry about damaging it. Wear protective clothing and especially gloves and a helmet.

Since the majority of falls are at a slow speed (usually while trying to negotiate an obstacle or tricky line on uneven terrain), practice falling at that speed. From a stand-still position (trackstand), allow the bike to fall to one side or the other. With your feet on the pedals (no cheating), put the inside pedal in the down position so it makes contact with the ground first. As it does, keep your hands on the grips and continue to fall, letting the outside of your calf touch next. Continue to "roll" up onto your thigh and side or back. The main thing you want to avoid is putting your arm out to break your fall. The end result of that tactic can be a broken collar bone, especially at high speed. Also, resist the temptation to break part of the fall with your elbow. Practice this from both sides until you're comfortable with the idea.

Going off the front is usually more dangerous than a side fall because your head is the first thing in line with the ground. Therefore, you have to get it out of the way first. To practice front falls, or "rear wheelies," you might want to look for something like a sand volley ball court or beach to absorb your fall.

Ride toward the cushioned area and lock the front brake until the back end of the bike comes up and you're looking at the sand. Do this a few times so you're comfortable with the feeling of going over. When you're ready, allow yourself to go over the handlebars, without letting go of them. Tuck your head in, roll, and let the back of your shoulder absorb the initial impact. Let your feet come off the pedals, unless you're comfortable with the bike tumbling with you.

Going off the back is probably the easiest to get used to because you usually have the opportunity to use your feet to help break the fall before falling backward. This kind of dismount is common when clearing obstacles or on steep off-road climbs where your body weight is too far back and the front end comes up. If you can, do a high wheelie with the front wheel, this is one of the best practice methods. If you are unable to do a wheelie, find a steep hill with soft ground and pedal up in your lowest gear combination with your weight back.

As you feel the bike coming back, get your feet off the pedals quickly and try to stand before falling back. Try hanging on to the bike to prevent it from tumbling back on top of you. If you can't maintain a standing position, turn your body so either side of your buttocks takes the brunt of the hit instead of your tailbone. At this point, you've probably let go of the bike, so tuck your arms in to your sides and roll back (flailing arms can get caught in the bike or something else as you tumble).

Sound like punishment? Perhaps. But this kind of practice can condition you to crash safely and avoid some injuries, so it might be worth a try.

Wheelies

Wheelies are a skill that you have to have a knack for, it seems. Some folks' sense of balance and equilibrium inhibits their willingness to lay back that far without falling. But, it's not difficult to wheelie several inches, enough to help clear an obstacle.

For most students, a low-gear combination of the small chainring and the largest or second largest freewheel cog will work. Rest your weight back on the saddle and pedal hard as you pull up and back on the handlebars. If this doesn't work, try a lower gear and compress the front tire or suspension fork. When it rebounds begin pedaling and transferring your weight to the rear.

If all else fails, find a long and fairly steep (grassy) hill and climb it in a low enough gear to bring the front wheel up off the ground. Experiment with moving your weight back until you can keep the tire off the ground. This will accustom you to the sensation of riding with the wheel up, even if only for short distances and "low altitude."

Sustaining a wheelie takes balance and control of the rear brake. Apply the rear brake to counteract the forward motion of pedaling to keep the wheel up. This is the part that takes some talent.

The Trackstand

Named after the maneuver utilized by velodrome racers to stall their forward motion as a tactic in pursuit racing, the trackstand is a useful everyday skill that you should master. You can use it to keep from putting your

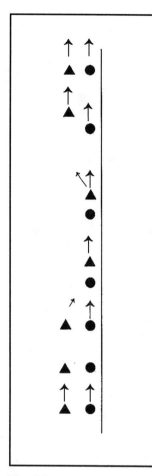

Fig. 6.6a.

foot down at traffic lights and stop signs, and for navigating through tight areas or rough terrain. Mastering this skill mainly requires good balance and a lot of practice.

Track riders turn the front wheel in toward the upward slope of the track and position the pedal on that side at the one o'clock (power) position. As the bike rolls back from the incline, the rider applies forward motion with the inside pedal to counter it. A small and slow rocking motion is created. You can simulate this on most streets that have a drainage crown (hump in the center). Turn the front wheel into the slope and pedal against the roll-back motion with pedal pressure.

As you control the back and forth movement, you will also need to add slight control to the brakes. It's probably easier to try it seated first because standing creates a higher center of gravity, making balance more precarious.

Remember to apply pedal pressure with the inside foot. The outside foot will tend to pull you away from the slope and the forward resistance. If the road has no crown, you will need to steer the front wheel left and right to maintain balance with the crankarms almost parallel (you will still need to apply a little forward pressure). When using the trackstand, especially in traffic, be sure that you have pre-selected a gear that you can pedal away in.

6.6 PARTNER & GROUP RIDING

Police cyclists will often ride in traffic with one or more partners. For reasons of safety, as well as to serve as an example to the community, officers should be able to ride both single file and side by side with ease. Transitioning from one to the other is an important skill intended to prevent collisions between riders. Above all, transitioning requires communication between riders.

Legally, riding two abreast is allowed in most states under most circumstances. There may be exceptions, so check local statutes and ordinances before riding alongside another cyclist. Riding more than two abreast is illegal and should be reserved for those special events when activities may require it.

Riding side by side is relatively safe. When the road narrows or high speed traffic is too close, it may be necessary to transition to single file. The outside rider makes the primary move. The first step is to communicate the move to the inside rider. Simply saying "single file" should work. This is necessary so that the riders don't overlap wheels and fall. Ideally, the outside rider accelerates slightly and moves to the right. The inside rider ceases pedaling, or even brakes slightly, to allow room for the first rider to merge. After being advised of the upcoming merge, the inside rider must first check behind to make certain it is safe to slow down. A collision could occur if another cyclist or vehicle is following too closely behind the inside rider. Once the inside rider has determined it's safe to slow, a simple "okay" or "go" should be said. (Figs. 6.6a, 6.6b).

When making the transition from single file back to double echelon, it is equally important that the rider who will move verbalizes the intent to move. The crucial error to avoid when riding single file or making lateral movements is overlapping wheels. If the front wheel of the rear rider overlaps the rear wheel of the front rider, the rear rider must quickly move back to avoid a collision or fall. If the front rider makes a lateral movement that causes wheels to touch, the rear rider will likely lose balance and crash. Movements of the front wheel allow a rider to balance. By diverting the wheel another direction or obstructing movements that help the rider balance, a crash may result.

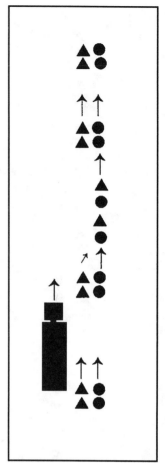

Fig. 6.6b.

Group Etiquette

Taking part in organized group rides is a fun way to get additional practice on your bike. Most organized group rides are rated according to difficulty as they pertain to speed, distance, terrain, and traffic. For your maximum enjoyment, and as a courtesy to others, select only those rides for which you are prepared. Introduce yourself to the ride leader and tell the ride leader if you plan to deviate from the ride. Following is a list of basic etiquette you should exercise when group riding:

Maintain spacing between other cyclists: Normally ride at least 1-2 bike lengths behind the cyclist ahead of you. Closer spacing for purposes of "drafting" is acceptable for experienced, mutually consenting cyclists. Never draft another cyclist without their knowledge and permission. Allow greater than normal spacing between bikes when ascending or descending a hill.

Ride at a steady pace without swerving: Every cyclist in a group bears some responsibility for those behind them. All riders should maintain a steady pace and ride in a straight line without swerving from side to side. Never follow another cyclist so closely that your front wheel overlaps the rear wheel in front of you. If your wheels should touch, you will abruptly lose steering control and you will probably fall sideways to the pavement.

Call out road hazards: Riders in the front of a group should warn those behind of hazards ahead, such as rocks, potholes, sand, gravel, glass, or oncoming traffic, and should make every effort to steer smoothly around the obstacles.

Generally ride single file: Ride single file unless traffic and road conditions and local statutes permit riding two-abreast safely. Be sure to exercise the proper communication outlined earlier in this chapter when moving into two-abreast and single-file positions.

6.7 TECHNICAL CYCLING—POINTS TO REMEMBER

Gears

Your bike has gears to make riding easier, faster, and more efficient. Use them! Learning to properly use your gears will allow you to have more fun and use much less energy. For police cyclists, not knowing how to use your gears correctly is like driving a police car that is stuck in overdrive or low. Either way you just don't move the way you want to. Using your gear system properly certainly won't take all of the effort out of riding, but it will definitely make it easier. Experienced cyclists are constantly changing gears to keep pedal forces low and pedal speed reasonably high. Inexperienced riders change gears "only when they have to !" Do what smart cyclists figured out long ago: learn how your gears work, then discover when to spin and when to "power through," based on the surface and terrain you are riding. By doing so, your police bike will be less fatiguing and you will enjoy your bicycling experiences more than ever before.

Braking

Mountain bike patrol officers must be in constant control of their bikes. They must be able to stop instantly while remaining upright and be able to do so in any weather or surface conditions. Proper body positioning upon the bicycle and proper hand positioning on the handlebars and brake levers are important. Of these, the rider's position on the bicycle is the most crucial.

Quick, controlled braking requires the use of both brakes, particularly the front brake. The front brake is the most effective brake when trying to stop quickly. As the bike comes to a stop, the rider's weight pitches forward, putting a much heavier load on the front tire and a reduced load on the back tire. This decreases the effectiveness of the rear brake. Many cyclists are afraid to use the front brake, having been warned of the danger of flipping over the handlebars as weight shifts toward the front wheel. While this is a possibility if incorrect braking and positioning are used, the cyclist using proper body position and a proper amount of brake input can achieve effective and controlled braking.

When a cyclist attempts to enact an unplanned or panic stop, from a high speed, the laws of inertia and momentum must be overcome using the law of gravity. When the need for a panic stop is recognized, the cyclist must immediately stop their pedals in the 3 and 9 o'clock position, while lowering their posture upon the bike. This is done by sliding the buttocks back on the seat and over the rear axle, lowering the head and torso, and bending the elbows and knees for shock absorption. To maintain maximum control, riders should remain in contact with the seat. This position helps overcome the tendency of the bike to pitch forward.

In addition to proper body position, officers must also control their bikes with the brake levers and handlebars. Properly adjusted brakes, of the quality found on police mountain bikes, require only two fingers to apply the pressure necessary to make a panic stop. Two fingers allow for a more refined "feel" and more delicate control.

To make a proper panic stop, use both the front and rear brakes at the same time, while applying a bit more pressure to the front brake. Be careful not to apply too much or the weight will shift rapidly to the front tire and increase the likelihood of skidding. This is especially true on wet, slippery or sand covered surfaces. The rider must listen for the sound of skidding. If skidding does occur, reduce the braking input to the front brake to shift some weight back to the rear wheel. Do not let up on the rear brake; it will only aggravate the problem. Remember, a braking wheel that is rolling is safer and more efficient than one that is locked. "Locking up" the wheel should be avoided in a panic stop.

Trying to turn while doing a panic brake will be nearly impossible because the position of the body will not allow the lean necessary to turn the bike. To turn or steer, the cyclist must first release the pressure on the brakes.

Another braking problem police cyclists experience —often while riding in the rain or crossing wet surfaces —is wet rims. Wet rims reduce the efficiency of the brakes and require a much longer stopping distance. This can be dealt with several ways. First, as a defensive cyclist, reduce speed in congested areas where panic braking is likely to be necessary. Second, initiate planned stops well in advance, allowing extra distance. Finally, apply a little pressure to the brakes to cause the brake shoes to squeegee the rims dry before you are ready to stop.

Officers will find it helpful to use their brakes while making a tight U-turn. They must maintain pressure on the rear brake and pedal through the turn to sustain momentum. By pedaling throughout the turn, officers can maintain momentum and prevent a fall when the front wheel is turned sharply.

Obstacle Clearing & Other Riding Techniques— A Recap

Curb Hopping. Curb Hopping is the most common skill utilized on patrol aside from shifting gears. It is also the most common cause for bent parts and injured riders. Curb hopping can be practiced repeatedly on patrol.

Steps to follow:

1. As you approach the curb or other obstacle to be cleared, stand on the pedals with the crankarms parallel to the ground. You should be in a crouch position with your knees bent.

2. Pull up and back on the handlebars to raise the front wheel over or on top of the obstacle, while shifting your weight toward the rear of the bike to lighten the front end. At slower speeds you can use the power pedal technique to help lift the front wheel, but this is a little trickier at higher speed.

3. As the wheel clears the obstacle, shift your weight to the front of the bike and pedal through. If you don't shift your weight forward, the rear wheel will slam into the obstacle while supporting your body weight. This extra burden makes it harder to pull the rear of the bike up to complete clearing the obstacle, and eventually results in bent rims.

4. Have a pre-selected gear that will allow you to pedal easily once the front wheel has cleared the obstacle.

It is important to be aware of how much clearance your bike has between the large chain ring and the ground. You will find when clearing tall objects like logs or tall curbs that the big chain ring will drag on top of the obstacle when the front wheel touches ground on the other side. To successfully clear these objects, it is necessary to lift the rear of the bike with your feet in the toe straps while centering your weight over the handlebars (after the front wheel has made contact). Your other option is to get off and carry the bike over.

Climbing Stairs. Becoming proficient at climbing stairs can save valuable seconds while in pursuit of a suspect should stairs be encountered en route. The average bike officer can clear 3-4 steps; anything taller than that takes skill and a lot of practice, not to mention the correct tire pressure and tread design. As a matter of practicality, it is probably better to dismount and carry the bike up the stairs or choose an alternate route.

Steps to follow:

1. Stand on the pedals with the crankarms parallel to the ground. You should be in a semi-crouch position with your knees bent.

2. Pick the front wheel up as high as possible to clear the first two or three steps. Again, at slower speeds it is helpful to use the power pedal technique to wheelie the front wheel up and onto the highest step possible.

   a. Remember that your weight should be toward the rear of the bike as you do this.

   b. The gear should be low enough to allow you to pedal up the stairs.

3. When the front wheel comes down, you begin to pedal. You should be pedaling while standing. This may seem obvious, but it is common to see riders who seem to stop to admire the fact that they have cleared the first two steps before they remember to pedal. The result is usually an aborted mission.

4. As you begin to pedal, try to keep your weight biased toward the rear of the bike to lighten the front wheel. This helps it go over the next couple of steps instead of plowing into them.

5. Shift your weight forward as the front wheel meets the destination surface.

6. Mentally concentrate on the top of the steps. Be up and over the steps in your mind. Your brain must be three to four seconds ahead of your bike.

Descending Stairs.
Steps to follow:

1. Approach the stairs straight without wobbling the tire back and forth. Use the big chainring if possible to reduce chain slack and the possibility of the chain bouncing off of the chainring.

2. At the top of the stairs shift your weight back off the saddle and be sure that the crank arms are parallel to the ground.

3. Grip the bars firmly and be sure to have good control of the brake levers (usually two fingers on each lever will do). You will rely mainly on the rear brake in this maneuver.

4. Stand on the pedals (crankarms parallel to the ground in the 3 and 9 o'clock positions) with your knees bent and your arms flexed at the elbows. This position will allow your body to absorb shock comfortably as the wheels bounce from step to step.

5. You must maintain the panic brake position—the balance of your body weight is centered back off the saddle and somewhat over the rear wheel, as well as from side to side.

6. As you begin to pick up speed, keep it in check by modulating the rear brake, as it is the main stopper here. Too much front brake could cause a rider to go over the handlebars.

Any steering input will be magnified because of the steep angle of the bike, so make changes in direction gradually. Until you become comfortable with descending stairs, it is advisable to keep the front wheel perpendicular to the stairs as you descend.

Climbing hills and long grades efficiently will enable officers to perform job tasks when they reach their destination, and not be so tired and drained of strength that they are unable to defend themselves or apprehend a suspect.

Gear selection is most important to successful climbing and total familiarization with the bike's drive train is essential.

Climbing Hills.
Steps to follow:

1. Let your legs do most of the work, instead of having your entire body in motion burning up precious oxygen and generating lactic acid. Stay aerobic.

2. Pull straight back on the handlebars to transfer weight/power from your body down to the pedals.

3. Select gears that will allow you to keep a reasonably high cadence, say 80 to 90 rpm. This lets you "spin" as opposed to standing and mashing the pedals down, which uses far more energy.

4. Keep your torso in an upright position to allow the lungs to fully expand and facilitate easier, deeper breathing. Relax your upper body as much as possible to conserve energy. Tight shoulders, stiff arms, and a "death grip" on the handlebars all cost energy that could be better spent by your legs.

5. On long, steep hills, break the ride up into sections with a specific goal to reach for each section. Pace yourself to reach each goal (such as a sign post 100 yards ahead) and try to distribute your energy evenly through the climb.

Successful climbing requires developing good leg speed to maintain a higher rpm. This can be practiced on flat roads by pedaling in a low gear at 100 rpm and above. Speed is not important in this training exercise.

Partner or Group Riding. When riding as a group, there are basic and advanced transitions you should be aware of.

Transitioning from pairs to single file and back. First, lets assume you are riding in pairs during low traffic or on a wide shoulder.

Steps to follow:

1. Prior to initiating the transition, scan behind and give the signal to merge to single file by saying, "single file."

2. The outside rider maintains speed and moves right while the inside rider slows or ceases pedaling to make space for the outside rider to move ahead.

3. The front rider always holds speed and communicates speed changes, surface hazards, etc., while the rear rider avoids overlapping wheels.

Now let's assume you plan to change back to pairs.

4. Riders scan rear and communicate "double up."

5. The rear rider, previously the inside rider, accelerates to outside position or pairs position.

Transitioning from two pairs of riders to single file.
Steps to follow.

1. Riders scan and communicate "single file."

2. Pairs stay together, outside riders merge with inside riders, while inside riders allow space (in front) for each merging outside rider.

3. Riders continue to advise of hazards and speed changes while preventing overlapping wheels with the rider ahead.

4. Riders command "double up" and scan rear.

5. Forward rider and third rider (previously the outside riders) move left, while the inside riders accelerate to pair up.

Practicing these types of transitions will greatly increase your ability to modify these transitions to avoid hazards, traffic, obstacles and changing road conditions.

CONCLUSION

Technical cycling starts with the proper size bike for the cyclist, and ends with practice, practice, practice. Gearing well, braking safely, and effectively being able to clear obstacles, climb hills, ascend and descend stairs, and knowing how to ride with a partner and within a group is essential to being a knowledgeable and effective bicycle patrol officer.

Chapter Seven:
Patrol Procedures

Previous chapters explain the importance of following the rules of the road. Patrol procedures will not at any time try to undermine this philosophy. Patrol procedures will only encourage officer safety and the need to respond quickly to calls. It will hopefully give you information necessary to develop the tools to do just that.

We know there are calls that need a priority response — a response time that is as quick as possible. In a patrol car, this means possibly exceeding the speed limit, maybe running a red light, with the aid of emergency lights and sirens. There is no doubt that when responding to these calls, you must drive very defensively and take care not to get into an accident. Obviously, if you crash before you get to the call, you haven't done anyone any good. As a matter of fact, all you've done is tie up more officers to help you. The same goes for a bicycle officer — only tenfold! If you make a mistake or take an unnecessary chance, it could mean your life. No question about it — fight with a car and you lose! It is still necessary for the police cyclist to respond quickly to calls, but it is also necessary for you to be more careful. When going against traffic, crossing the street before an intersection, and so on, you must ride much more defensively than you ever dreamed of when you were in that patrol car. Be careful and get there in one piece!

7.1 Advantages and Disadvantages of the Bike Patrol

Advantages of the Bike Patrol

In your career as a police cyclist, you will discover a host of advantages over the bad guys. Following is a list of the most prevalent advantages of police cycling:

1. **The stealth advantage.** This is your number one advantage of being a bike cop. A bike enables you to ride up on a crime-in-progress without the players ever knowing you're there. It will just astound you. Hiding yourself also becomes much easier than with that big steel box.

2. **Faster respnse time.** In urban traffic, patrol cars are often tied up with traffic lights, one-way streets, stop signs, or rush hour. Many times you will get to the call, handle it, and be back in service before the patrol car can even get there.

3. **Foot pursuit is made obsolete.** This is like bringing a knife to a gun fight. Wherever the suspect runs, your bicycle can go. Bad guys know this and, on many occasions, will just give up.

4. **Better public image.** You become much more approachable on bike. No longer are you in this big, sterile, steel box. With a better image, more people know that you are actually human. This becomes nice when you're down and dirty fighting for your life, and the guy you just finished talking with about bike frames comes over to help you.

5. **Department benefits.** Bikes cost less at the pumps; there is lower cost per officer; less miles are put on patrol cars; and physically fit officers have less down time.

6. **Environmentally better.** No fuel consumption means no emissions.

Disadvantages of the Bike Patrol

Despite the many advantages, there is a down side to bike patrol.

1. **Less recognizable as a police officer.** Though this can work to your advantage (stealth), it can also work against you.

2. **Sometimes slower to reach calls.** Depending on the size of your district, time of day, and terrain, it may take you longer to respond to calls.

3. **Exposed to the elements.** If it's 100-degree weather with 98 percent humidity when you get to that call, you will probably be wiping the sweat out of your eyes. It can be a distraction if you have to apprehend someone or take somebody at gunpoint. Rainy, 38-degree weather can be likewise cumbersome. Neither situation is much fun, but it's just part of the job.

4. **Too much public relations.** Tourists will want to take their pictures with you, citizens may want to discuss your bike's componentry, or your captain may be sending you out on every kids rodeo duty he can find. All well and good, but it does get old after awhile.

5. **Other officer perceptions of the bike squad.** You are likely to receive a lot of negative comments about the bike squad, such as being called "prima donnas," "pretty boys" and the like. It's up to you how you handle these comments, but perhaps offering to take them out on a ride along to give them a taste of just how "easy" your job is may be an effective way to change their perceptions.

6. **Lack of cover.** Though your bicycle is a great crime fighting tool, it has a major drawback: it offers absolutely no cover. It's not hard to envision just how dangerous it can be in a shooting situation.

7.2 STOPS AND PURSUITS

Traffic /Vehicle Stops

In a patrol car, officers take traffic stops for granted. On a bicycle, it takes on a new meaning. You don't have a light bar or siren to assist you in getting that violator to the side of the road. But, there are some things you can do to help improve your effectiveness with this part of normal patrol.

Fig. 7.2a. Waving the car over and using an audible signal is your safest option

Fig. 7.2b. Contacting the car above the rear driver's side tire after the car has stopped

1. Attempt to make eye contact with the vehicle operator. Not only does this help you make the stop, you also know the driver sees you. Waving your arms seems to do the trick. (Fig. 7.2a). When you get the driver's attention, you can point him in the right direction to pull over. When pointing, make sure you use your index finger.

2. Assuming the car does not see you, you will need to make an audible sound. This can be done by yelling at the driver to "pull over," or by blowing a whistle.

3. As a last resort, if steps 1 and 2 don't work, and assuming you really want to pull this person over, you will have to make physical contact with the car. (Fig. 7.2b). Contact should never be made with a moving car—only make contact when the car is stopped. Also remember the following:

   A. Do not ride up to the driver's window.

   B. Come up to the left rear quarter panel by the rear tire.

   C. Gently tap on the panel with your knuckles— not your flashlight or baton.

   D. This will get the driver's attention and alert him of your presence.

   E. Have the driver pull to the side of the road.

   F. Place your bicycle on the sidewalk or to the far right of the shoulder. (Fig. 7.2c).

   G. Never put your bicycle in front of you or behind the car. Get your bike out of "harm's way."

   H. At this point, conduct your stop as you normally would.

Actual experience has proven that police cyclists can effectively make traffic stops.

Vehicle Pursuits

What if a car tries to get away? Vehicle pursuits can be fun! Nothing angers a motorist more than when some bicyclist catches them. When pursuing a vehicle, keep in mind the following:

1. Don't give up just because the car is faster than you.

2. Even though a motorist is trying to outrun you, many times they stop at the next traffic light, assuming you won't catch them before it turns green.

3. A fleeing motorist's attention is often on the rear-view mirror instead of on the road. The common result is an accident with another car or object.

4. Nothing is faster than a radio. Call other officers to help.

5. Just as with a motorized pursuit, continually weigh the risks you are taking with the reason for the pursuit.

As you can see, with a little effort, bike cops can be an effective traffic-stop tool.

Fig. 7.2c. Place the bicycle on the side before approaching vehicle

Suspect Contact
Two-Officer Stop:

A. **Contact Officer:** The contact officer will approach the suspect and dismount the bicycle. During the initial contact, the officer should place the bicycle between him and the suspect. (Fig. 7.2d). If the suspect becomes agitated, the contact officer can use the bicycle as a weapon by throwing the bicycle at the suspect or by dragging the suspect over the bicycle. If the suspect tries to walk around the bicycle, the officer can use the bike to block his forward motion. The contact officer should do all the talking to the suspect and maintain constant eye contact on him.

B. **Cover Officer:** The cover officer approaches the suspect with the contact officer, but from a different angle (however the terrain allows). Be careful not to place yourself in a cross-fire situation if the contact goes sour. Unlike the contact officer, the cover officer stays on his bicycle. The cover officer ratchets his power pedal into a power position. If the suspect decides to run, this officer's responsi-

Fig. 7.2d. Proper contact officer, cover officer position

Fig. 7.2e. Backing the suspect to the bike

Fig. 7.2f. Using the bike as leverage

bility is to begin the pursuit. The contact officer will join the pursuit as soon as possible.

C. Changing Roles: If during the contact the suspect decides he doesn't want to talk to the contact officer anymore, it is easy to change roles. The contact officer becomes the cover officer, and vice versa.

One-Officer Stop:

Follow step "A" for two-officer stop and wait for backup.

The Arrest:

A. The contact officer will take control of this situation.

B. Have the suspect turn around and place their hands on their head. (Fig. 7.2e). If they are cooperative, have them backup to the bicycle where you can reach over the bike and place handcuffs on them. If the suspect becomes agitated, your advantage is you can pull him backwards over the bicycle.

C. If the suspect is not cooperative, be sure to move the bicycle out of the way before approaching him. If you step in front of the bicycle, the suspect could possibly push you over your own bicycle. Unless the suspect is going to stand and fight, the cover officer should not leave the bicycle until the suspect is in handcuffs.

D. Another procedure is to have the suspect stand as flat as possible against a wall. Place the bicycle against the suspect with the chainring toward the wall and between his legs. (Fig. 7.2f). Then, place your foot against the chainring to push the bike against the suspect. The top tube will be about hip high on the suspect. If the suspect becomes agitated, this leverage will make it difficult for him to turn or run on you. If this method is used, the cover officer can dismount.

Take-downs

Take-downs are the part of the job that can be very risky. The chance of injury to you greatly increases whenever you employ any of these techniques. You also have to consider the degree of crime before you use a take-down. If your target is a ranting wino, you would not want to use a take-down. On the other hand, if the target is a rape, robbery, or murder suspect, then a take-down would be justified. Before employing any of the take-down techniques, be sure to discuss them with your department to guard against legal liability. Take-downs should only be used during pursuits or in high-risk situations. In high-risk situations, you must be assured that you have the upper hand or at least the element of surprise on your side.

In some jurisdictions, the bicycle use of force comes under the same category as using the baton. A baton is not considered lethal force, but it can kill. The bicycle also has this potential.

Types of take-downs:

1. **Verbal Request.** In some circumstances, you may want to try riding up along side the suspect and asking them to give up, before employing a take-down. This can sometimes accomplish the same objective without physical contact.

2. **Power Slide.** This is intended to strike the suspect in the ankles. When doing this maneuver, hold the rear brake as tight as possible (and until the maneuver is complete), lean to one side (preferably the non-power side), plant the down-side foot on the ground and push hard on the up-side foot. Aim the rear tire toward the suspect and BOOM! The rear tire will hit the suspect's feet and knock him down.

NO LONGER TAUGHT

3. **Over the Top.** Ride up to the suspect and simply reach out and grab them. Push him/her forward and down. Ninety-nine percent of the time, the bicycle will fall away. This type of take-down can be the most fun, but it is the hardest to master and is subject to the greatest amount of injury.

4. Half Dismount. Do a half dismount, then using the motion of the bicycle, step off and drive your shoulder into the suspect.

The previous take-downs are generally considered near the higher end of the force continuum. Practice them with both a suspect and the training cop wearing protective gear, such as helmets, mouth guards, Redman® pads or other full contact-type padding. Practice power slide take-downs using a traffic cone or similar object in place of a "suspect." *In any case, a take-down should not be attempted in a real situation unless enough practice has been had to ensure the safest and effective take-down.*

7.3 NIGHT PATROL

Night patrol can expose a bike officer to a different world and a unique set of hazards. Night patrol obviously differs because of darkness and visibility problems. Additional hazards include:

- Invisibility in traffic, especially during foul weather.
- Shadows and darkness hide surface hazards.
- Shadows and darkness effect depth perception and make obstacles more dangerous.
- Darkness makes it more difficult for back up officers to find you.
- Darkness amplifies sounds, especially for the "bad guys."

Those officers who work night shifts know that they are that much more stealthy and effective at night. They also understand that:

> *It is more important to always ride with a partner at night.*

Know your beat. When working at night it is very important to know every inch of the beat and where the normal surface hazards are. Slow down at night; surface hazards change daily. Take time to see, hear and sense more of what is happening around you. Use shadows to your advantage. Stay in the shadows and use them for concealment whenever possible. Some departments use a different uniform for night patrol. They use an all dark uniform, which enhances their ability to use shadows for concealment when necessary.

Be visible. It is very important that night patrol officers have all of the legally-required lights and reflectors. Those may not be enough. It is strongly suggested that patrol bikes have at least a 10 - 15 watt headlight, with a rechargeable battery. These headlights enable officers to ride with speed and not overrun the headlights. They also offer the advantage of totally illuminating suspects as officers approach them. This is something "everyday" bicycle lights just can't do!!

Some departments equip their bicycles with LED flashers for increased conspicuity. Others have their officers attach them to their duty belt. While these lights can be effective in traffic and can even help back-up officers find officers in a dark alley or back yard, they are not without hazard. One large city bike officer was approached by a known gang member and asked why he doesn't wear one of those flashing "targets" like they do in the neighboring city. Now that you know what the other side thinks, it may be better to leave the flasher attached to the bike.

Much has been said about using reflective material on patrol uniforms. It is often misunderstood. Retro-reflective materials work when exposed to a direct light source. They cease working when the light source is more than 3 degrees from direct. If you shine a light on a reflector and stand directly behind the light, that is the brightest it will get. As you move more than three degrees away from the light the reflection will diminish to nearly nothing. If your suspect is sitting on a street light pole, an officer wearing reflective material will be "reflective" to the suspect. A person sitting on the ground, far more than 3 degrees will have no advantage at all. Some officers fear wearing any reflective material. Placing retro-reflective material only on the back of the uniform will help bike officers stay visible in traffic. The badges many officers wear on their breast are often curved and shiny, with many oblique reflective surfaces. These shiny surfaces may face toward street lights and other light sources and in reality create a bigger tactical problem than do reflective cloth tape. What a perfect target! A truly tactical night uniform would incorporate a cloth emblem badge.

Officers need to be particularly aware of the sounds that they, their bike and their equipment make. Many officers use ear plugs with their radios. They also keep pedaling slowly to eliminate the ratcheting noise made by a coasting freewheel.

In summary. Night patrol requires an officer to pay more attention to what they're hearing, where they're riding, what they're wearing, and the noise they're making. Paying attention to these details will make for a stealthier and more effective night patrol.

7.4 OFFICER SAFETY & FIREARMS TRAINING

There have been numerous applications of lethal force over the last several years by bicycle officers. It has ranged from 70-yard shots to stop a person with an automatic weapon to a shot from 5 feet away while being shot at. IPMBA's firearms course details the hazards and safety issues involved with being a bicycle officer. It deals with things such as cover vs. concealment, the necessity of fitness, communications between officers and high-risk scenarios. The firearms qualification course is designed to simulate actual situations bicycle officers encounter and how best to survive them.

Hazards

So what are some of the hazards of being a bicycle officer? The most obvious is the bicycle officer's ability to get extremely close to criminal activity before being recognized. As previously mentioned, the element of surprise is what allows bicycle officers to be extremely successful but, by getting so close, they are at a greater risk of physical confrontation. If a suspect is not willing to give up, they basically have two choices: fight or flight. By getting so close to a suspect, it reduces the chance for flight. That leaves only fight. Additionally, since bicycle officers typically patrol urban areas, the number of contacts and arrests they encounter are great. Suspects in higher crime areas also tend to be more street-wise and because of prior criminal activity, may have more to lose if they get caught.

A bicycle officer is extremely vulnerable while on the bicycle. A patrol officer working a motor vehicle has got 3,000 pounds of steel surrounding him, which offers immediate cover. The patrol vehicle can go 0 to 60 mph in about 6 seconds, and can operate in reverse. It can also be maneuvered with one hand allowing officers to utilize their radio to ask for assistance if necessary. A bicycle officer has 30 pounds of aluminum below him, which does not provide concealment, let alone cover. A bicycle officer will not reach 25 mph in 6 seconds or even 10 seconds and has no reverse. A bicycle officer must use both hands to effectively maneuver the bicycle, making it difficult to radio for assistance, should it be needed.

The final major hazard deals with the recognition of the members of the bicycle unit. Bicycle cops are the most feared officers by most drug users and dealers, as well as gang members. This is because of the bicycle's effectiveness. However, this also puts the bi-

7.4a. Don't give up your position with your helmet

cycle officer at greater risk of ambush. Because of this, some specialized tactical training is encouraged.

It is clear the job of the bicycle officer is a dangerous one, but with training this increased risk can be minimized.

Cover vs. Concealment

Since bicycle cops are among the most vulnerable officers due to their exposure, certain tactics should be employed to help reduce their risk. Knowing the difference between cover and concealment is paramount. Cover can be an object of size and consistency that provides an officer protection from projectiles. Concealment is an object of size and consistency that provides an officer with a location to hide, though it does not provide protection from projectiles. Cover is an engine block, a telephone pole, or a concrete wall. Concealment is a bush, a fence or a garbage can. A bicycle officer should always be aware of his surroundings and the existence of potential cover. Where cover is not available, concealment should be pursued. It is impossible for a bicycle officer to continually have available cover while on patrol. However, locating cover should be paramount in an officer's mind when approaching a potential threat.

If a bicycle officer is moving in to make an arrest, his approach should involve cover. If a bicycle officer is involved in a suspicious person contact, he should still be thinking cover. Cover officers should set up near cover and, because left-side bicycle dismounts are the most natural, the cover should be to the left.

If approaching a suspect that may pose a threat, the bicycle officer should at least utilize concealment when cover is not available. This will at least limit the subject's opportunity to react to the bicycle officer's presence.

There is no tactical advantage to remaining in an urban area that is absent of cover. Leaving yourself exposed should be a last resort option. It can usually be avoided by choosing your location for contact. If a suspect is moving through an area where cover is not available, the bicycle officer may choose to delay contacting the suspect for some distance. This is one more advantage of the bicycle. It's stealth-like capability can enable you to maintain your surveillance, while continuing to track the suspect. Don't forget to remove your helmet when cover is being utilized. Keeping the helmet on will only telegraph your position early. (Figs. 7.4a, 7.4b).

Communications

Communications between bicycle officers is an absolute must. It is equally important to keep the dispatcher informed of any contacts or criminal activity. Most patrol officers realize the increased risks involved with being a bicycle officer and will move in the bike officer's direction if they know a contact or an arrest is going to be made. Bicycle officers should develop a plan for any contact or arrest situation. In time, things begin to fall into place with a partner, but even the smallest things should be vocalized. If an arrest is going to be made, there should be a #1 officer and a #2 officer. The #1 officer should communicate what actions he will take such as "He's walking southbound on the sidewalk. I'll take the sidewalk and you take the street. I'll try to contact him near the set of cars so that you'll have cover." It can take as little as 15 seconds to develop a plan and communicate it. This arrest will go much smoother than if nothing was said. In the event of a higher risk contact, or arrest, it may be more intelligent for both officers to obtain cover then take verbal control of the subject thereby minimizing the risk of injury to both officers.

7.4b. Removing your helmet can help you blend into the environment

Where there is no cover available, the use of marked patrol units is recommended. Remember, discretion is the better part of valor. Most bicycle officers will take a few chances, but they should be minimized whenever possible. Whenever there is any kind of a contact it is the responsibility of the cover officer to avoid a crossfire. The cover officer can usually move more easily than the contact officer.

Understanding Risks

Probably the most difficult thing to do for a bicycle officer is to slow down. If there is a hot call in the area, most bicycle officers will ride hard to get to it. This is the last thing a bicycle officer should do. Riding hard to get to the area is reasonable but always remember to save some energy for the "bad guys." These hot calls are the greatest risk for bicycle officers for three reasons. First, many of your motor patrol colleagues are also traveling extremely fast to get to the call. A patrol vehicle will beat a bicycle in a collision every time. Second is the potential for an ambush exists. The criminal may want the bicycle officer to rapidly enter an area without looking. Third, the bicycle is very vulnerable. It can be extremely deadly to ride into the area where shots are still being fired.

Bicycle officers should move into the area cautiously, utilizing whatever cover and concealment is available. Bicycle officers should monitor whatever is taking place, but wait for patrol vehicles whenever possible before moving in.

Fitness Levels

Physical fitness is important for all police officers, but it is an absolute necessity for bicycle officers. Most non-bicycle using police officers exert themselves very little en route to a call, so they are relatively rested in the event of a physical confrontation. Bicycle officers exert themselves going to the call, but they must have enough energy left for that physical confrontation. It is completely reasonable for a bicycle officer to arrive on a call, but remain a short distance away until they have re-energized themselves. There have been bicycle officers seriously injured for not doing this.

The next question is what affect does physical exertion have on an officer's ability to fire a weapon? Where an officer has exerted himself, but within the confines of the body's natural resources, his shooting will usually be improved. Where an officer goes beyond his body's natural resources, his shooting will be negatively affected. It is, therefore, extremely important for the bicycle officer's natural resources to be as high as possible and for each bicycle officer to realize his limitations.

FIREARMS TRAINING COURSE

The purpose of the following firearms training course is to bet-ter prepare bicycle officers for handling a lethal force encounter should one arise. Officers will develop skills for approaching scenes using cover and concealment and learn how to dismount quickly and make it safely to cover. Officers are taught to adapt to the feeling of firing their weapon while still wearing their gloves and other equipment that is unique to bicycle patrol. With practice, bicycle officers will be able to use their firearms proficiently after physical exertion and in situations where the bicycle is involved. (Figs. 7.4c, 7.4d)

7.4c. Practice while wearing your helmet, gloves and glasses is extremely important

7.4d. Padded bike gloves make a big difference when gripping your firearm

A Firearms Training Course video is available through the International Police Mountain Bike Association. Please see the "Resource" section of this book.

Each officer will need the following equipment:
- Police bicycle
- Helmet
- Gloves
- Eye protection
- Complete uniform, including jacket
- Bullet-proof vest
- 2 targets (consistent with Qual targets)
- 63 rounds of ammunition
- Multiple sources of cover

Course rules: There are several rules that must be strictly adhered to during the firearms training course.

Rule #1: No live fire exercise may be done outside the presence and supervision of a range master/firearms instructor.

Only IPMBA certified instructors that are also certified range masters/firearms instructors can conduct this course. It is the Police Cyclist Instructor's responsibility to ensure proper operation of the bicycle and proper mounting and dismounting techniques. The range master/firearms instructor's responsibilities involve course safety and proper use of firearms.

Rule #2: Firearms are not to be drawn or fired from a moving bicycle.

There is absolutely no tactical advantage to firing from a moving bicycle. It limits acceleration and maneuverability, therefore, prolonging the officer's exposure. There is also a reduced chance of firing accurately, which poses too great a risk to the public.

Rule #3: All courses of fire will be demonstrated in person or by use of a video prior to any live fire exercises.

Because there are risks involved in any firearms training, and those risks are enhanced by the presence of bicycles, it is invaluable for bicycle officers to visually see what they will be doing. It removes the unknown and, therefore, improves the overall safety of the course.

Rule #4: All courses of fire requiring dismounts will be practiced a minimum of two times prior to the live fire exercise.

Repetition is a necessary element to all training. Not only are skills improved, but practice helps ensure a clear understanding of the course of fire prior to the course of fire itself.

Rule #5: Additional range rules can be instituted at the discretion of the range master/firearms instructor.

Because each range is different and each department's policies are unique, additional range rules may be necessary.

18-Round Course of Fire

This course of fire is designed to help officers understand the need for training and how strenuous aerobic activity effects their shooting. It also gives the instructor the opportunity to evaluate the skill and fitness levels of individual officers.

The course of fire.

1. Officers will put up a target then return to the 10-yard line. They will not have their bicycle, helmet or gloves. Eye protection will still be necessary. Officers will unholster their firearm and load it with 6 rounds. They will then reholster and secure the firearm. Officers using semiautomatic weapons will only place a clip with 6 rounds in the magazine well, without taking the gun out of the holster. After the clip is secure in the weapon, the officer will, on the command of the Range Master, remove the weapon from the holster and chamber a round. If decocking is necessary, it will be done at this time.

   Upon the command, "Draw and fire 6 rounds ... Fire," the officer will draw his weapon and fire all 6 rounds at the target. After shooting is complete, the officer will go to a low ready position and scan, then reholster an empty weapon. When the firing line is clear, as designated by the Range Master, the officer will go forward to the target and mark the holes with a RED marker. **TIME: 8 seconds.**

2. Officers will remain at the 10-yard line. Upon the command, "Load your weapon," the officer will load 6 rounds as described above. Officers will put on gloves and helmet and mount their bicycles 4 feet to the right of the target. They will place themselves in a "power pedal" position. Upon the command, "Dismount left, draw and fire 6 rounds ... Fire," the officer will dismount on the non-power side (left) and fire all 6 rounds at the target. After firing, the officer will go to a low ready position, scan, then

reholster an empty weapon. When the Range Master clears the firing line, the officer will go forward and mark these 6 holes with a BLUE marker. **TIME: 8 seconds**

3. At the 10-yard line, officers will again reload with 6 rounds as described above. The officers will mount their bicycles ride to a point 1/2 mile from the range and return at a minimum of 15 mph. Riders should be approximately 1 minute apart with the faster riders out front. They will ride to the 10-yard line, dismount, draw and fire 6 rounds without command. These 6 holes will be marked with a BLACK marker upon command of the Range Master. **TIME: 8 seconds**

Following this first course of fire, the instructor should review these targets. Using the RED marker, the instructor should connect the 6 red bullet holes. This is the baseline grouping and will be used for comparison with the two other sets of bullet holes.

The instructor should then connect the 6 blue holes using the BLUE marker. This grouping, when compared to the first set, should be consistent in size. Each officer's skill level and groupings should not be compared to other officer's targets. If the BLUE grouping is larger than the RED this indicates that the officer's performance is negatively affected by the bicycle's involvement. Additional training is suggested.

The instructor should then connect the 6 black holes using the BLACK marker. This set of 6 holes will provide the instructor with information on the effect of physical exertion on shooting quality. This final set of 6 bullet holes should be somewhat smaller that the first two. An officer whose fitness level is acceptable will usually be affected positively by the physical exertion. The exertion, as long as it is within the confines of the body's resources, will steady the officer and improve their focus. Conversely, if the BLACK grouping is similar to or larger than the RED & BLUE groupings, it indicates that the officer's fitness level needs to be improved.

45-Round Course of Fire

1. With a fresh target in place, officers will put their bicycles at the 3-yard line. Bicycles should be parallel to the target with the power side to the target. With a fully-loaded weapon, officers will take an interview stance behind the bicycle. Upon command, officers will draw their weapon, simultaneously kick their bicycles toward the target, and fire 3 rounds. They will then retreat two steps, while still facing the target. All officers on the firing line will try to back up the same amount of distance. This will be repeated at the 5-yard line for a total of 6 rounds. **TIME: 5 seconds**

2. At the 7-yard line, officers will mount their bicycles and get in the power pedal position. Upon command, the officer will draw and fire 3 rounds. This will be repeated for a total of 6 rounds. **TIME: 5 seconds**

3. Again at the 7-yard line, officers will stay seated in the power pedal position. Upon command, officers will exit/dismount on the left side and fire from a standing position next to their bikes. This will be repeated on the right side of the bike for a total of 6 rounds. **TIME: 5 seconds**

4. Officers will place barricades at the 10-yard line. Officers will then stay seated on their bikes and get into a power pedal position. Upon command, officers will dismount on the left side of their bikes and seek cover to the left. Officers will then fire 3 rounds from the right side of that barricade. This exercise will be repeated to fire from the right side barricade for a total of 6 rounds. **TIME: 8 seconds**

5. Officers will then move the barricades to the 15-yard line and place their bicycles at the 50-yard line. Upon command, officers will ride forward to the 15-yard line, do a half dismount and with disregard

for the bike, seek cover to the left barricade. There, officers will fire 3 rounds from the right side of that barricade. This will be repeated to the right barricade and firing from the left side of that barricade, for a total of 6 rounds. **TIME: 15 second**s

6. Officers will return to the 50-yard line and, starting in a power pedal position, ride forward to the 15-yard line. Officers will do a power slide dismount then draw and fire 3 rounds. **TIME: 15 seconds**

7. Again from the 50-yard line. Officers, upon command, will ride forward to the 15-yard line, do a slide stop dismount behind the left barricade, then draw and fire 3 rounds from the right side of that barricade. This will be repeated to the right side barricade firing from the left side of that barricade for a total of 6 rounds. **TIME: 15 seconds**

8. Officers will then move their barricades to the 25-yard line. This final phase of fire will start at the 50-yard line. Upon command, officers will ride to the 25-yard line, do a power slide dismount and seek cover to the left. Officers will fire 3 rounds from the right side of that barricade. This will be repeated to the right barricade, firing from the left side of that barricade for a total of 6 rounds. **TIME: 18 seconds**

In evaluating this course of fire, instructors will need to know how well each officer normally shoots. There will likely be a dramatic difference, with most officers being negatively affected by the use of the bicycle. Officers who normally shoot in the 90s can shoot as low as the 50s. Officers who have difficulties shooting under normal circumstances will be even more negatively affected. This shows the urgency for actual firearms training directed towards bicycle officers. Officers who have shot the course on more than one occasion show improvement each time and those who have shot once a month for 6 months should be at least nearing their normal shooting.

Each course of fire simulates actual common occurrences for bicycle officers. Officers should be instructed to fire this course as realistically as possible.

Bicycle Firearms Qualification Course

DISTANCE	10-yd. line
ROUNDS	6 RDS
TIME	8 sec.
SCENARIO	No helmet, gloves, or bicycle * Use RED marker

DISTANCE	10-yd. line
ROUNDS	6 RDS
TIME	8 sec.
SCENARIO	Helmet, gloves and eye protection; power pedal dismount; draw and fire * Use BLUE marker

DISTANCE	10-yd. line
ROUNDS	6 RDS
TIME	8 sec.
SCENARIO	1-mile ride at 15 mph+; dismount; draw and fire * Use BLACK marker

Now Replace target

DISTANCE	3-yd. line
ROUNDS	3 RDS
TIME	5 sec.
SCENARIO	Bike between officer and target; interview stance; kick bicycle towards target; draw and fire

DISTANCE	5-yd. line
ROUNDS	3 RDS
TIME	5 sec.
SCENARIO	Same as previous scenario

DISTANCE	7-yd. line
ROUNDS	3 RDS
TIME	5 sec.
SCENARIO	Power pedal position; draw and fire

DISTANCE	7-yd. line
ROUNDS	3 RDS
TIME	5 sec.
SCENARIO	Same as previous scenario

Place cover at the 10-yard line both left and right of line of fire.

DISTANCE	10-yd. line
ROUNDS	3 RDS
TIME	8 sec.
SCENARIO	Power pedal dismount; seek cover left; draw and fire from right side of left cover

DISTANCE	10-yd. line
ROUNDS	3 RDS
TIME	8 sec.
SCENARIO	Power pedal dismount; seek cover right; draw and fire from left side of right cover

Move cover to 15-yard line, both left and right of line of fire.

DISTANCE	15-yd. line
ROUNDS	3 RDS
TIME	15 sec.
SCENARIO	Ride from 50-yd line to 15-yd line; half dismount to right cover; draw and fire

DISTANCE	15-yd line
ROUNDS	3 RDS
TIME	15 sec.
SCENARIO	Ride from 50-yd line to 15-yd line; half dismount to left cover; draw and fire

DISTANCE	15-yd. line
ROUNDS	3 RDS
TIME	15 sec.
SCENARIO	Ride from 50-yd line to 15-yd line; power slide dismount; draw and fire

DISTANCE	15-yd. line
ROUNDS	3 RDS
TIME	15 sec.
SCENARIO	Ride from 50-yd line to 15-yd line; power slide dismount; seek cover right; draw and fire

DISTANCE	15-yd. line
ROUNDS	3 RDS
TIME	15 sec.
SCENARIO	Ride from 50-yd line to 15-yd line; power slide dismount; seek cover left; draw and fire.

Move cover to the 25-yard line, both left and right of line of fire

DISTANCE	25-yd. line
ROUNDS	3 RDS
TIME	18 sec.
SCENARIO	Ride from 50-yd line to 25-yd line; power slide dismount; seek cover right; draw and fire

DISTANCE	25-yd. line
ROUNDS	3 RDS
TIME	18 sec.
SCENARIO	Ride from 50-yd line to 25-yd line; power slide dismount; seek cover left; draw and fire

TOTAL: 63 RDS

CONCLUSION

Bicycle patrols have many elements to them, and a vital element is the actual "police work" that is involved. Being on a bicycle changes the officer's approach toward stops, pursuits, night patrol, and especially the use of their firearm. The unique training needs and patrol considerations of a bicycle officer must be addressed for a successful bicycle patrol unit.

CHAPTER EIGHT:
BICYCLE LAW ENFORCEMENT

8.1 THE CASE FOR BICYCLE LAW ENFORCEMENT

The recruit was seated behind the wheel of the Training Academy patrol car. This was his twelfth week of training and, though nervous, he felt he was ready for anything. The directions from his instructor had been to handle whatever developed in this training scenario. This role play training was a bit more intense than previous ones because it was being conducted on the edge of a residential area. Nearby residents were stopping to watch the action. While the recruit was waiting for the scenario to unfold a young man on a bike rode by the recruit in the training car and continued past the scarlet red stop sign, pedaling all the way. The recruit sat waiting patiently, until the instructor approached the car and told him that he had just "failed" the scenario. The scenario "offense" had been the bicycle violator that rode in front of the recruit. "But I was waiting for some real police work," explained the recruit. "That was just a guy on a bike." The instructor asked the embarrassed trainee, "If the police don't enforce the bike laws, who will?"

In most police academies in the U.S., this scenario would never occur. If bicycle laws are covered at all, it's usually as part of the traffic code, which can be dry and boring! If recruits see a bicyclist in role plays, they are usually armed with surprise weapons or loaded down with drugs. Rarely, if ever, is any emphasis put on simple bicycle violations.

As a result, it is rare to see a police officer stop a bicyclist for a traffic violation, even though cyclists are subject to many of the same rules as motorists. Whatever the reasons, cyclists and motorists are not always treated equally. Police officers are charged with enforcing the law. When they ignore cyclists committing violations, they are not doing their job—and they are missing an opportunity as police cyclists to protect them, other road users, and the public at large.

Did you know...

- Bicycle crashes are the number three reason for hospital emergency room admissions nationwide. Number one is car crashes. The U.S. Consumer Product Safety Commission (CPSC) reports that in-line skating crashes only recently passed bicycle accidents to take the number two position.
- Bicycle accidents cause more deaths and injuries to children than either crime or disease.
- One recent study showed that, based on miles traveled, the bicycle fatality rate is more than three times as high as the automobile fatality rate, and the injury rate is more than forty times the rate for motorists.

So what can you do?

Road safety for bicyclists and motorists comes from incorporating the Elements of Traffic Safety—The Four E's: Engineering, Encouragement, Education, and the **ENFORCEMENT** of traffic laws for all road users. This includes bicycle offenses!

Past efforts to reduce the number of bicycle crashes have focused solely on educating young cyclists, and other road users, in schools and at bicycle rodeos. Education has primarily covered the basic rules of the road. *Engineering* bikeways and widening roads can help reduce car/bike crashes. The *encouragement* of proper behavior is an important part of the equation. Even with those in place, though, if no one enforces the rules, behavior won't reflect safe practices. Of all the elements of traffic safety, bicycle traffic enforcement has the greatest potential to reduce car/bike crashes and save lives.

Bicycle traffic enforcement and bicycle safety education go hand-in-hand, with enforcement providing the backbone to the bike safety that is taught. The power of enforcement is the power of reinforcement.

How Can Police Officers Benefit From Enforcement?

It allows them to:

- Achieve voluntary compliance with the laws.
- Identify and correct violators and repeat violators.
- Reduce the number of bicycle-related crashes.
- Reduce the injuries and deaths resulting from these crashes.
- Effect behavioral change in the community.
- Reduce the $1,000 per person, per year in public costs that result from U.S. bike crashes. It's estimated that public costs resulting from these bicycle deaths and injuries are as high as $8 billion dollars annually.

8.2 WHY DON'T POLICE ENFORCE BICYCLE LAWS?

Police officers know that it's their job to enforce laws equally. They also know that enforcing traffic laws can prevent accidents, save lives and money, and prevent needless heartbreak. So, why don't many officers enforce bike laws? Here are some reasons officers around the country have given, and some responses to those reasons.

Peer Pressure. "Bike laws aren't real crime." "I'm a crime fighter and I only have time for real police work." "I don't want the other officers to think I'm afraid to do real police work." Enforcing traffic laws and preventing crashes, injury and death are REAL police work—especially when it effects children. Don't let peer pressure and old stereotypes keep you from doing the right thing.

Social Pressure. "Citizens say to me, 'Why aren't you catching robbers or burglars?'" "People say to me, 'Haven't you got something better to do than pick on little kids?'"

What officer has never heard a motorist ask them similarly ridiculous questions? Do you allow this to stop you from enforcing other traffic laws? Of course not! What officer has never heard a complaint about those "crazy bicyclists" who disregard red lights and stop signs, terrorize pedestrians on the sidewalks and create general chaos in the community? If the police don't enforce bike laws, who will?

Police Administration. "Not a department priority." "My Chief doesn't want me out stopping bikes."

Has your chief ever said not to stop bike violators? Or, are you just making an assumption? Supervisors and administrators are influenced by the same outdated stereotypes that influence most street officers. They too require education and sensitizing. Chiefs are swayed by public opinion. If the community supports bicycle enforcement to reduce crashes, it's a good bet your chief will support it, too!

Prosecutor/State's Attorney/Courts. "My calendar is crammed and you bring me this?" "This matter is too petty."

You agree with every decision your prosecutors and judges make, right? Sure! Do you stop doing your job simply because the prosecutor doesn't want to do theirs? Keep in mind that judges and prosecutors can be swayed by a small group of reasonable and knowledgeable people. The influence and impact of the group MADD is a perfect example. Remember, enforcement can take place, without involving the attorney or the courthouse, through written and verbal warnings, impounding unlicensed bicycles, etc.

Time. "I don' t have time for trivial matters. Some days we don't have time to get to dinner because it is so busy." "I only have time for real crime."

Do you have time for other self-initiated traffic enforcement? Some departments are so busy they don't. Usually those departments have traffic divisions that do nothing but traffic enforcement. If you have time to do other traffic enforcement, you have time to enforce bike laws. Do you have time to write "more important violations" like parking tickets, expired registration or equipment violations? Do these "more important violations" have more potential to prevent crashes and save lives, or do they merely fit your stereotype of what police officers are "supposed" to do? Ask yourself which enforcement activity is more likely to save lives...parking tickets or bike stops?

Remembering Your Childhood. "Police never stopped me on my bike when I was a kid. I did the same stuff and I'm still here!" "That's not what police do." "I don't want to scare a kid, or make them cry. That doesn't leave a good impression of the police."

What you remember from your childhood has a name—history! Police equipment, technology and philosophies are different today. When most officers were young, they rarely saw police officers in schools. Today they are commonplace. Traffic (and the patience of drivers) is much worse today than it was when you were young. Ignoring a dangerous violation is never better than risking having someone dislike you. If the goal of the contact is to educate the cyclist and enhance their safety, the risk of leaving a bad impression is minimal.

Waiting for the Big One. "If I tie myself up on this petty stuff I won't be clear to back up my partner or respond to emergencies or crimes in progress." "I want to be available when the BIG one comes in."

What officer has never had an emergency call come in while they are on a traffic stop? Figuring out how to clear is rarely a problem on simple violations. If this is your attitude toward all self-initiated activity, it's likely you don't have any. If this is how you feel, why didn't you join the Fire Department? Waiting for the BIG one is what they do!

They Will Only Hurt Themselves. "If they want to ride their bicycle like that, they will only hurt themselves if they get in an accident." "Stupid, careless people get what they deserve eventually."

The plain and simple truth is bicycle/motor vehicle crashes never involve "just" the cyclist. Somebody else is always affected. It will always affect someone else physically, emotionally or financially...sometimes all three. Often, totally error-free motorists suffer stress, guilt, and anxiety for years afterward. Many end up defending themselves in court and spending thousands of dollars to do so. This is especially true if the crash involves a child.

Have you ever had to notify a parent that their child has been killed in an accident? Does the parent's reaction lead you think that no one else was affected? It's usually pretty gut-wrenching and emotional. Death notifications are police work, too. Which kind of police work would you rather do...bike stops or death notifications? Remember that the next time you think or say, "but they will only hurt themselves."

8.3 WHY POLICE SHOULD ENFORCE BICYCLE LAWS

Most police officers would like to think that the job they do makes a difference...that they have helped make the community better and safer. Traffic law enforcement is one area where police can have a measurable impact. With officers periodically taking a few minutes, or even seconds, to deal with bicycle-related violations, enforcement can result in a noticeable reduction in bicycle crashes and injuries.

Up until now, in far too many communities, bicyclists have been allowed to operate in traffic while violating basic traffic rules—and the accident rates reflect it. Bicyclists are 40 times more likely to be injured in traffic than a motorist.

In the past, many officers thought bike enforcement wasn't important enough for them to spend time on. They thought teachers were solely responsible for bike safety by educating children. Some believed that engineers were most responsible by designing and building bike paths and lanes. It is time for police to get involved and add the crucial element of enforcement, with a firm, fair and consistent commitment to enforcing targeted violations.

Bicycle traffic management and accident prevention requires no more than a basic knowledge of traffic law, being alert to the targeted violations of bicyclists, and taking appropriate action. This is especially true for police cyclists who reap the additional benefits of a safer cycling environment.

Targeted Violations

The following violations account for the majority of bicycle/motor vehicle collisions. Concentrating bike enforcement efforts on them will prevent many injuries and save lives.

Target Violations for Bicyclists:
- No headlight at night
- Wrong-way riding/riding against traffic
- Disobeying traffic control signals or devices (stop signs and other posted signs)
- Failure to yield right-of-way (e.g., exiting driveways, alleys, improper turns, etc.)
- Improper change of course (e.g., unexpected left turn from the right side of the street)

Targeted Violations for Motorists:
- Failure to yield right-of-way (e.g., left turns in front of cyclists, pulling out from stop signs, right turns on red)
- Improper passing (e.g., passing too close or cutting off cyclists)
- Driving Under the Influence of Alcohol

Types of Enforcement

Enforcement (or reinforcement) can take several forms:

- Citation or arrest
- Verbal warning (education opportunity)
- Written warning or parental notification
- Positive reinforcement (free food coupons, movie tickets, or department trinkets)
- Verbal warning (as a reminder) on the PA when unable to make a stop or when en route to another call. Penalties can include:
- Fines
- Community service
- Mandatory attendance at a bicycle safety clinic
- Other local programs

If your unit decides to sponsor a bicycle safety class, local bicycle clubs may be able to provide instructors if police personnel are unable to teach the class.

Increasing Bicycle Enforcement (A.K.A., Attitude Adjustment)

There needs to be a change in attitude among street officers, supervisors and administrators before bicycle enforcement will be recognized as a valuable and vital use of police time. Attitudes can be changed through training, experience, re-defined department goals, and modeling.

So, what are some of the things that influence a department or an individual officer toward improved bicycle enforcement?

Time. Time spent in training: basic academy training and field training, which will break the old stereotypes; in-service training in roll call; or specialized training courses in bicycle traffic management. The League of American Bicyclists has a video titled "The Law is for All" made for roll call training. Contact the League at 202-822-1333 about obtaining a copy.

Money. Money spent on training or special enforcement efforts (e.g., overtime paid to officers working bike enforcement in problem areas or part of a special program).

Significant Emotional Event (SEE). Exposure to, or involvement in, a critical incident may provide one of the strongest, longest-lasting attitude adjustments. Recognizing victims who look like your children, parents, or yourself can cause officers to experience a SEE. Some experience a SEE when they realize the violation or behavior is done by their children, or they chose regularly not to enforce it. Feeling involved makes a lasting impression upon officers.

Administration Prioritization and Support. Setting bicycle enforcement on the agenda as a department priority. This enables the administration to send a message to supervisors and then they send it on to the rest of the department.

Veteran Officers. Vets are responsible directly and indirectly for the attitudes of new officers coming into the department. New recruits will seek to imitate, and win the approval of, vets. Getting capable and respected vets to stop a few bicycle violators (and put it on the radio) will give the new officers, and maybe even a few of the older "fence sitters," the idea that good cops can enforce bike laws without losing respect or credibility.

Spin-Offs. Bicyclists who break traffic laws often break other laws as well. Officers who stop bicyclists report recovering a number of stolen bikes as well as drugs. They also make a number of arrests. In urban areas many drug couriers are using bikes to elude police or avoid vehicle forfeiture.

Bicycle Enforcement Start-Up Strategies

If your department has never done specialized bicycle enforcement or never sent a bicyclist to court, you need to consider some special strategies and considerations if the new program is to succeed. The effectiveness and acceptance of your new program can be improved by employing certain strategies.

Administration. Get the police administration behind the program. Any program will run more smoothly if everyone knows it has the Chief's blessing and the line supervisor's are prepared to support it.

Program Coordinator. The program coordinator has to be someone who wants the program to work. Preferably this person is a highly motivated, self-starter. Nothing kills a program faster than a coordinator who doesn't care about the program or its success.

Courts and Prosecutors. Starting a program that will bring new juveniles into the system is likely to face resistance from the courts and prosecutors. Solicit their support and concerns before implementing any new program. They may want to set a minimum age for referral to the court (e.g., no one under 14 goes to court) or agree to make attendance at a violator seminar an option to court appearance. You will have greater success working with these people ahead of time, rather than trying after the fact to deal with the confusion a new program may create.

Policy and Procedure. Before starting out, print up special bicycle citation books which have bicycle identification information and allow them to be used as a written warning or summons to violator seminars. Some departments will print basic bicycle safety information on the back of the violator's copy. It is also necessary to develop form letters to notify parents and obtain safety materials. It's necessary to establish procedural guidelines for record-keeping, enforcement, bicycle impoundment, and so on. Your department may find it helpful to put this in standard policy form in the police policy manual.

Education. Education is a must for administrators, line supervisors, and the officers responsible for enforcement. They must understand the procedures, target violations, and, in some cases, have their "attitudes adjusted." The public also must be educated, which can be done through the media, schools, Parent-Teacher Organization meetings, civic groups, fliers, city newsletters, utility bill "stuffers," local cable channels, city message boards, etc.

Media/Publicity. Don't surprise the public with the new enforcement campaign. Let them know what is about to happen and why. Tell them what the targeted violations are up front and encourage voluntary compliance. If the program is run fairly and consistently, and they don't feel ambushed, the public will be very supportive.

CONCLUSION

B icycle law enforcement is crucial. It saves lives, promotes safe cycling, and leads to the recognition of the bicycle as a legitimate vehicle—something that bicycle patrol officers already know. Bicycle law enforcement is a critical step for bicycling to gain greater prominence as a way for individuals to both commute and recreate—which is, of course, good for individuals from the physical, psychological, and environmental point of view. Do officers realize they can play such a role in the future of bicycling?

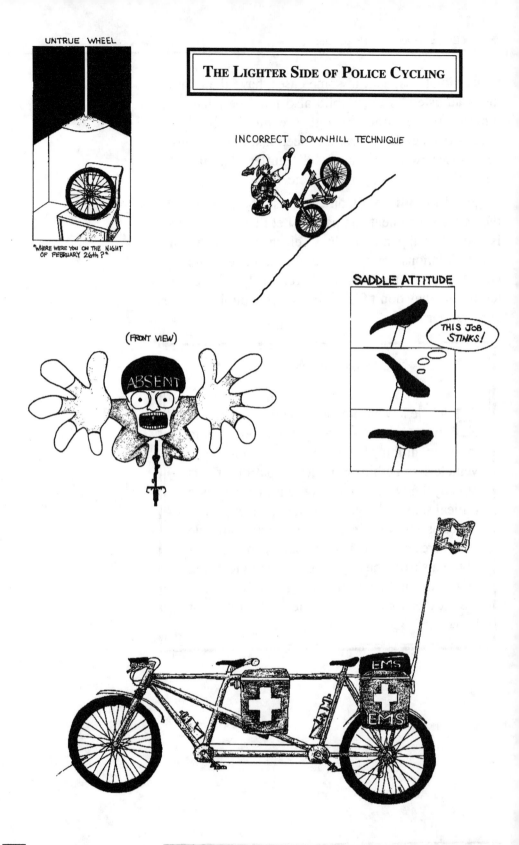

ABOUT THE AUTHORS

KIRBY BECK has been in law enforcement for more than 21 years. He is a police pfficer in Coon Rapids, Minnesota and has been a bicycle officer since 1991. As an L.A.B. Effective Cyclist Instructor, Kirby (PCI #2)—along with Allan Howard—created the initial IPMBA Police Cyclist Course. An authority on vehicular-style cycling, Beck moonlights as a training consultant with the U.S. Department of Transportation, and teaches bicycle safety, education, and enforcement around the United States.

ERIC DAVID BLAIR has been a U.S. Army Instructor, Alameda County Deputy Sheriff, State University Police Cyclist, and police association representative. Although he prefers not to discuss politics or sports, Blair describes himself as a "radical centrist" who prefers to participate rather than observe. He considers himself an adventurer who is pursuing many projects in writing, cycling, Aikido, diving, cosmology, and other forms of travel.

STUART J. BRACKEN has been with the Tacoma (Washington) Police Department for 11 years. He has been teaching throughout the state for 4 1/2 years, and nationally for 2 1/2 years. While serving on the International Police Mountain Bike Association (IPMBA) Board of Directors, he has been assigned to the downtown bicycle squad for 5 years. During that time he has made over 2,000 arrests as a police cyclist.

GARY GALLINOT has 19 years of general police experience. He implemented the bicycle patrol program at the Santa Monica (California) Police Department in

1990. He currently supervises the six police cyclists and eleven community service officers who make up the Santa Monica Bike Unit. He is on the California State Peace Officers Standard and Training (POST) bicycle patrol task force, and is currently developing a State Certified curriculum for bicycle patrol training. Sgt. Gallinot is presently enrolled in an MBA program, holds a B.A. degree in Public Management and maintains an A.A. degree in Police Science, and has served on the IPMBA Governing Board.

J. LEITH HARRELL has been with the Deland (Florida) Police Department for many years. He frequently writes articles about police cycling for the IPMBA news letter, and is an active supporter of law enforcement cycling.

ALLAN HOWARD is a bike patrol officer and a 13-year veteran of the Dayton, Ohio Police Department. He is a former USCF racer, one of the founding members of IPMBA, and Police Cyclist Instructor #1. Allan was elected Chairman of IPMBA in 1992 and has been re-elected to that position three consecutive times since. When not actively engaged in police work, Allan can be found motor pacing transit buses and semis.

ANDY MACLELLAN is a 13-year veteran and current Corporal in charge of the Baltimore County (Maryland) Police Department's bicycle patrol. He has been a member of the IPMBA Governing Board since 1993. He is also currently serving on the Maryland State Governor's Bicycle Advisory Law Enforcement subcommittee.

JOE MARTIN is currently a Sergeant with the Hayward (California) Police Department, but in his 20-years in law enforcement, has been a civilian, military, reserve and campus law enforcement officer. He has been active in many police related associations, including being a former board member of the California Law Enforcement Association (CLEA), and he is currently serving on the IPMBA governing board . He also served on the committee that developed the California bicycle patrol training safety standards. Martin is an active IPMBA Police Cyclist instructor and regularly bikes 25 miles to work.

GARY MCLAUGHLIN has been a bike officer with the Sacramento Police Department for more than 6 years. Gary was among the officers who attended the Certified Police Cyclist Course the first time it was offered in the nation. He has served on the IPMBA Governing Board.

GENE MILLER is a veteran bike officer with the Tacoma (Washington) Police Department. He is the Chairman of the Education Committee of IPMBA, and one of the original architects of the Police Cyclist Instructor. program.

DAVE ROSS has been with the Hayward (California) Police Department since 1979. He began his career as a Community Service Officer and in 1981 became a sworn officer. Officer Ross has been assigned to the Traffic Bureau since 1984. He is in charge of the bicycle safety program , which he teaches to elementary school students in Hayward, and oversees bicycle safety rodeos in the area.

TOM WOODS has been a police officer with the Denton (Texas) Police Department since 1969. He has been a Sergeant in field operations since 1986, and in 1990, he established the department's first bike patrol. He is a founding member of IPMBA and has served as both IPMBA Secretary and Vice Chair. In 1994, he established the first police mountain bike patrol in the former Soviet Union as part of Project Harmony Law Enforcement Exchange, in Peterozavodsk, Karelia, Russia. A USMC Vietnam veteran, Woods is known in the Arctic Circle as the "Father of Russian Police Mountain Biking." (Really!) He is an avid mountain biker, road biker, bike buyer, seller, swapper, and avid "I wish I could afford that bike" dreamer.

PARTS OF A MOUNTAIN BIKE

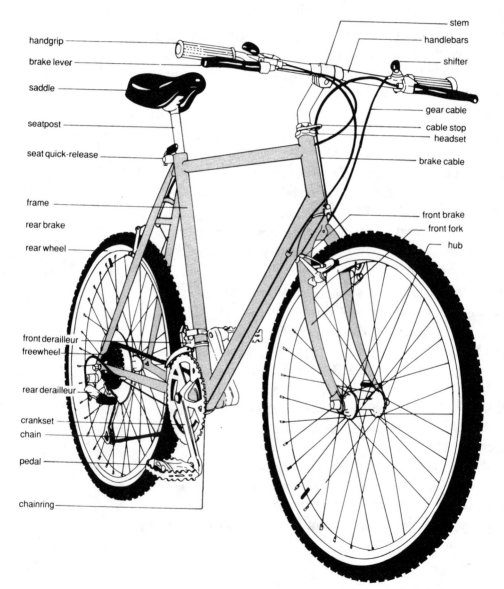

stem

handgrip

handlebars

brake lever

shifter

saddle

seatpost

gear cable

cable stop
headset

seat quick-release

brake cable

frame

front brake

rear brake

front fork

rear wheel

hub

front derailleur
freewheel

rear derailleur

crankset
chain

pedal

chainring

front wheel

GLOSSARY

All-Terrain Bike (ATB): A synonym for mountain bike.

ANSI: American National Standards Institute; a helmet safety approval rating like the Snell rating.

Barrel Adjuster: A threaded bolt with a hole through its center and a special nut designed to be turned by hand, allowing for fine adjustments of cable tension and compensation for pad wear.

Beat: The area rhythmically patrolled by an officer.

Bicycle: A two-wheeled, chain-driven vehicle propelled by pedaling.

Bike Lane: A marked lane on a roadway or highway that suggests where cyclists should commonly ride.

Bike Path: A marked pathway, separate from the roadway, for bicycles and other non-motorized vehicles.

Bike Rodeos: An obstacle or skills course, sponsored or promoted by a police department, which encourages community interaction and bicycle safety. Usually involves police cyclists.

Bonk: Riding so long and/or so hard that one loses the desire and ability to continue physical exertion. Fitness, hydration, and nutrition determine when a rider will bonk. The term is sometimes used to mean the same as "hitting the wall," however the latter term more often connotes that an individual has had it for the day. Bonking can sometimes be reversed by rest, hydration, or eating. In an athletic or recreational setting "bonking" will mean less than a record performance. In a public safety context, pushing yourself to this extreme could be deadly for the public safety cyclist, his or her fellow officers, or a civilian. Unlike a bicycle race, in this business, the real competition begins after you cross the finish line. During CPR or an arrest, there is no time to bonk.

Bottom Bracket: The part of the frame at the bottom of the down tube and the seat tube where the cranks, axle, and bottom bracket bearings are located.

Brake Boss: 1. A threaded metal stud on a bike frame, to which the brake arm is attached with a bolt. 2. A supervisor who tells you when to take brakes.

Brake Bridge: The small tube on the frame to which the brake unit is attached.

Brake Cable and Cable Housing: The brake cable transmits force from the hand levers to the calipers; the cable housing supports the cable and permits it to be properly routed.

Brake Pad: The replaceable rubber pad which fits into the brake shoe and makes contact with the rim of the wheel. Pads are held in place by brake shoes. (Where brakes live).

Cable Anchor Bolt: The bolt that secures the brake cable to the lower caliper.

Cable Hanger: Small fitting bolted or welded to the frame or handlebar stem. It provides an anchor point for the brake cable housing.

Calipers: The "arms" that hold the brake pads and move when the handle bar levers are squeezed.

Campagnello: Sometimes called Campy for short. Italian bike component maker. Very famous. Very good. Very expensive. One of the "Big Three."

Campy: Bike fan speak for Campagnello.

Cantilever Brakes: Most often found on mountain bikes, touring bikes and tandems, because they are capable of providing tremendous stopping power when properly adjusted.

Chain Sock: 1. An old piece of footwear used to clean your bike chain. 2. When grease from your chain marks your clean sock: A clear indication your socks are too high.

Chain Suck: When the chain jumps off the chain wheels and becomes jammed between the frame and chainrings.

Civilian: A.K.A. "Silly-Villain." The reason we exist.

Clip-less Pedals: 1. Replaces standard pedals, or those with toe clips, with system integrating, specially designed shoes and pedals that the cyclist can "clip" together. When in this fixed position, cyclists can pedal on the down stroke and upstroke for much more efficient cycling.

Code 3: Responding to a life and death emergency call or crime in progress with siren and red or blue lights turned on. Conversationally, it may mean "really fast."

Conspicuity: Devices that increase the wearers signature, illumination or ability to be seen in darkness or low light situations.

Crank User: An excellent up hill cyclist. A.K.A. "Crankster."

Crash 'n' Burn: A ghastly collision or crash which could involve spilled DNA samples.

CSPC: Consumer Product Safety Commission.

Dishing: Dishing refers to the art of truing the rear wheel so that the rim on the poser side of the wheel is closer to the right. This is unlike front wheels, which are trued so the wheel is centered on the hub. Dishing is necessary to allow room for the freewheel. (Not to be confused with dissing, the practice of not showing enough respect).

Dismount: Exiting your bike. There are two kinds of dismounts; intentional and un-intentional.

Dog: Sworn enemy of letter carriers and cyclists.

Dropouts: The end of the front forks and the rear portion of the frame where the axle of the wheel is attached.

Dual Pivot Sidepull Brakes: Dual pivot brakes are nearly identical to single pivot ones, except for the obvious extra caliper pivot point. Some component makers claim it provides more mechanical advantage (leverage) because of the location of the pivot points, but the calipers themselves are also much beefier, which might account for more of their increased efficiency.

Dual Suspension: Bike with both front and back suspension equipment. A.K.A. fully suspended.

Effective Cycling (EC): The name of a popular education program of the League of American Bicyclists, based on the book "Effective Cycling" by John Forester.

Effective Cycling Instructor (ECI): A person who meets the stringent requirements of the League of American Bicyclists to conduct EC classes and certify cyclists.

Event Horizon: The minimum braking/reaction time of a given obstacle. The highest point along a planned route.

Face Plant: A nasty crash where the rider hits face-first.

Fat Tire (slang): A mountain bike, as opposed to a touring bike which has a skinny tire.

Front Suspension: Front shocks or other front fork suspension.

Fully Suspended: Both front and rear suspension.

Groin Plant: The worst thing, aside from death, that could happen to you during a crash or near crash.

Headtube: The short tube which the stem and the fork are held in. This is where the manufacturer's name is most prominently displayed. The top tube and the down tube are connected to the headtube.

Honed: Also, totally honed or honed to the max. Having great skill.

International Police Mountain Bike Association: (IPMBA)—pronounced "eye-pim-ba." A division of the League of American Bicyclists.

LAB: The League of American Bicyclists. Formerly the League of American Wheelmen, LAB is the parent organization of IPMBA.

Mechanic: A person who knows how to fix your bike, if you don't.

MOJO: Good luck charm. Sometimes affixed or otherwise attached to handlebars.

Mountain Bike: The whole reason we're writing this book. A mountain bike is an excellent community policing tool.

Off-The-Back (OTB): Falling behind. Not keeping up. Proper use: "Dude, you were totally OTB -- better luck next time!"

Over-The-Bars Club: Exclusive club open only to those who have experienced much pain when involved in a major crash -- usually rewarded with laughter from other members.

Pasta: Starchy noodles best served with sauce. Excellent source of carbs.

Peddler: 1. Bike rider. 2. Annoying door-to-door salesperson.

Pitcher: A bike whose front brakes work great, but rear brakes mysteriously didn't function.

Pivot Bolt: Attaches the brake unit to the frame, passing through the brake calipers pivot point.

Police Cyclist (PC): A person who has the requisite training and experience as mandated by IPMBA and has been certified by IPMBA after completing a standard course of instruction and passing written and on-bike skills testing.

Police Cyclist Instructor (PCI): A certified PC and working bicycle officer who has passed the stringent requirements of IPMBA to enable them to conduct IPMBA Police Cyclist training and certify students.

Police Cyclist Instructor Candidate (PCIC): A PC who has met some but not all of the PCI requirements and is working with a PCI towards gaining PCI certification.

Primum Mobile (Lat): The source of motion, the mainspring, the primeval force.

Public Safety: 1. Any public safety service such as police, fire and/or medical services. 2. Term inclusive of the police and fire services, or in some places used in place of law enforcement. For instance, the City of Sunnyvale, California, has a combined police and fire department called the Department of Public Safety. In Texas the state police is referred to as the Department of Public Safety.

Quick Release: A really neat little device, which if properly used, can make repairing a flat tire much easier. Also found on many seat posts as well. The only downside to quick releases are people too stupid to make sure the things are in their closed position before riding off. Such persons often inflict damage upon themselves. These people then find attorneys who have never heard the expression "caveat emptor" and as a result file ridiculous law suits endangering this simple and functional piece of engineering.

Rear Suspension: Any bike that has a suspension device that allows rear wheel movement.

Return Spring: Located behind the calipers with the pivot bolt running through it, held in place by little notched tabs on the calipers. Makes the brakes open when the hand levers are released.

Roadie: Human who rides one of those skinny-wheeled, drop handlebar contraptions (not practical for police use).

Shimano: Japanese bike component maker with biggest chunk of the market share.

Shimano Pedaling Dynamics (SPD) or "Spuds": A family of recessed mountain bike cleats, which allow maximum pedalling efficiency without interfering with one's ability to walk or run when off the bike. Many companies are now making variations on the same theme.

Slime: 1. Green semi-liquid tube sealant which will increase the time between flats.   2. The driver of the car that just cut you off.   3. Some of our "customers."

Snell: Another helmet approval rating.

Spin: Also "good spin". Selecting a gear which allows the rider to easily pedal at around 80 to 90 rpm for maximum efficiency. Bike racers often spin over 100 rpm, tourists somewhat slower.

Toe or Toe In: Facing forward and looking down on a set of properly adjusted brakes, you will notice they appear very slightly "pigeon toed." By having the front or leading edge of the brake pad closer to the rim it facilitates more efficient braking. Often when a brake "chirps" or squeals—thus announcing the arrival of an otherwise stealthy officer—it is in need of being toed in. This term should not be confused with what you do to the cars driven by unlicensed drivers.

Trials: A set of obstacles, or the "most difficult" part of a trail.

Tune-up: Inspection and readjustment of your bike.

UBP: Uniformed Bicycle Patrol.

VO$_2$ Max: The amount of oxygen the body absorbs during maximum exertion. Interesting concept which has application to those who are training for athletic endeavors. Like bonking, VO$_2$ max is something the public safety cyclist should avoid while on duty.

BIBLIOGRAPHY

Anacapa Sciences, Inc. A Study of Bicycle-Motor Vehicle Accidents — Identification of Problem Types and Countermeasure Approaches. National Highway Transportation Safety Administration (NHTSA), 1977.

Beck, Kirby. The Minnesota Peace Officer's Guide to Bicycle Traffic Management. Outdoor Empire Publishing, 1991.

Bicycling Magazine. Complete Guide to Bicycle Maintenance and Repair. 310 pages. Rodale Press, 1990.

League of American Bicyclists. Bicycle USA Magazine. League of American Bicyclists, 1995.

Bridgestone. The 1994 Bicycle Catalogue from Bridgestone. 73 pages. Bridgestone Cycles, 1994.

Cuthbertson, Tom. Anybody's Bike Book. 236 pages. Ten Speed Press, 1990.

Forester, John. Effective Cycling. 599 pages. MIT Press, 1993.

Hunter, William & Stutts, Jane, C. Bicycle Law Enforcement Manual. North Carolina Department of Transportation, 1994.

Institute of Police Technology and Management. Bicycle Law Enforcement Manual. University of North Florida, Jacksonville, 1987.

International City Manager's Association (ICMA). Sourcebook-Community Oriented Policing: An Alternative Strategy. ICMA, 1992.

The International Police Mountain Bike Association (IPMBA). IPMBA News. League of American Bicyclists, 1995.

Kelly, Charles. Richard's Mountain Bike Book. 191 pages. Ballentine Books, 1986.

National Pedestrian Safety Program. Walk Alert Program Guide. National Safety Council, 1989.

Nealy, William. Mountain Bike! A Manual of Beginning to Advanced Technique. Alabama: Menasha Ridge Press, 1992.

Pleven, Arlene. Cycling. 184 pages. Fodor's Sports, 1992.

Rochlin, Gene. Scientific Technology and Social Change. 403 pages. Scientific American, 1989.

Sloane, Eugene. The Complete Book of Bicycling. 4th edition. 542 pages. Simon & Schuster, 1988.

U.S. Department of Transportation. Law Enforcement Pedestrian Safety. DOT HS 808 008. Office of Driver and Pedestrian Programs, 1993.

Vander Plas, Robert. The Mountain Bike Book. California: Bicycle Books, Inc., 1993.

INDEX

NOTES

NOTES

NOTES

NOTES